AF516894

YOGA EDUCATION

YOGA EDUCATION

A Textbook

Dr. Kamakhya Kumar

Senior Faculty
School of Yoga and Health
Dev Sanskriti Vishwavidyalaya
Haridwar

SHIPRA

All rights reserved. No part of this work may be reproduced, stored in a retrieval system or transmitted in any form or by any means, electronic, mechanical, photocopying, recording or otherwise without the prior written permission of the copyright owner and the publishers.

(First Published in India in 2012)

Rs. 995, US$ 33

ISBN: 978-81-7541-622-2

2024 Impression, PoD

Yoga Education: A Text Book

© Dr. Kamakhya Kumar

Published by:
SHIPRA PUBLICATIONS
LG 18-19, Pankaj Central Market,
I.P. Ext., Patparganj, Delhi 110092, India
11 47322068, 22235152/6152; 9650028065
info@shiprapublication.com
www.shiprapublication.com

Dedication to—
My Parents:
Smt. Indu Devi Singh
&
Sri Sachidanand Singh

Foreword

I first met Dr. Kamakhaya Kumar when my search for psycho-spiritual literature emanating from a deeper quest for understanding the larger purpose and meaning of life took me to library of Dev Sanskriti University at Haridwar. Awestruck by the unique stature of the university and feeling quietude in the ambience, I got interested in understanding the activities of various departments. It was at the School of Yoga and Health where I learnt about Dr. Kamakhya's work and participated in the discussions on the subject of Yoga.

Scientific understanding of the discipline of Yoga is deeply rooted in the Indian culture and heritage. Yoga has been practiced in our country for several thousand years. With changing times, understanding of the discipline of yoga has undergone some change. The theories and concepts, though remain the same, the application has changed due to increased understanding and appreciation. During the early Sixties, yoga *asanas* were taught for physical fitness or for beautifying the body. Later on as the thrust of yoga changed, it came to be seen as a way to reduce stress and anxiety, and relax the mind. With the emergence of Meditation, it became a way of finding mental peace. Yogic practice of achieving mental calmness is widely prevalent now. Many organizations and individuals have adopted the yogic structure and created their own brand of yoga that addresses the needs of many people today.

In modern times, a vast majority of people driven by their ambitions and endless desires find themselves thrown into a conflict in relation to their work, family and society. This gives rise to an internal imbalance and one strives to attain inner peace and harmony. This is where understanding and practicing yoga is very useful. But the number of experts engaged in propagating and teaching yoga is rather small to cater to the needs of a vast majority of people. In this context, the present Volume makes a useful addition as it serves as an excellent guide-book for the yoga teachers who are keen to learn, and to teach Yoga methodically with an in-depth knowledge.

The book sets out to give insights into the nature and meaning of yoga and clarifies misconceptions that are widely prevalent. Altogether in nine chapters, the book systematically and scientifically explains the traditions and types of yoga; yogic practices; the role of yoga for a healthy life style; and above all the different methods of teaching. It is therefore visualized to be a comprehensive resource as it covers all the aspects of yoga teaching that may be necessary to be learnt by a teacher. With an earnest hope that the book will be accessed by a large number of yoga teachers who are able to make use of it in their journey to be master trainers, I send my best wishes.

Prof. (Mrs.) Neelam Sood
National University of Education Planning
and Administration, New Delhi

Contents

Preface vii

List of Figures xi

Introduction **1**

I. Introduction to Tradition of Yoga **5**

- Yoga: Its Meaning and Importance 5
- History of Yoga 11
- Schools of Yoga 23
- Jñān Yoga 24
- Bhakti Yoga 28
- Karma Yoga 32
- Rāja Yoga 35

II. Introduction to Hath Yoga **39**

- Shatkarma 42
- Āsana 43
- Prānāyāma 45
- Mudrâ-Bandha 49

III. Introduction to Pātanjal Yoga **52**

- Concept of Chitta and its Modifications: Chitta Vritti 52
- Introduction to Pātanjal Yoga 54
- Astānga Yoga 56

IV. Introduction to Human Body and Mind **59**

- Skeletal System 59
- Muscular System 60

- Digestive System 61
- Respiratory System 62
- Circulatory System 62
- Skin 62
- Nervous System 63
- Excretory (Urinary) System 63
- Reproductive System 64
- Endocrine System 64
- Effect of Yogic Practices on Human Body 65
- Human Mind and Role of Yoga in Mental Health 66

V. Yoga and Health Care 71

- Concept of Health and Disease in Yoga 71
- Yogic Practices for Common Man 73
- Yogic Management of Common Disorders 75

VI. Role of Yoga for Healthy Lifestyle 84

- Healthy Life Style and its Importance in Healthy living 84
- Yoga and Healthy Lifestyle 88

VII. Yoga and Education 91

- Role of Yoga in Education 91
- Role of Yoga towards Personality Development 95

VIII. Methods of Teaching Yoga 98

- Teaching Methodology in Yoga 98
- Evaluation in Yoga Teaching 120

IX. Yoga Practices 124

Common Instructions for the Practice 124
Preparatory Practices 125
Sūrya Namaskār 133
Meditative, Cultural and Relaxation Āsana 139
Prānāyāma Practice 153
Śatkarma Practice 158
Practice Leading to Meditation 163
Special Relaxation Technique: Yoga Nidrā 166

Index 171

List of Figures

Pagewise

1. Initial Position / 125
2. Padanguli Naman / 126
3. Gulfnaman / 126
4. Gulf Ghūrnan / 127
5. Janunaman / 127
6. Janu Chakra / 128
7. Janu Falak Akarsan / 128
8. Ardhatitali / 129
9. Purnatitali / 129
10. Shronichakra / 130
11. Mustikabandh / 130
12. Manibandh Chakra / 131
13. Kehuni Naman / 131
14. Skandhachakra / 132
15. Griva Sanchalan / 132
16. Pranamasana / 133
17. Hastotthānāsana / 134
18. Padhastāsana / 134
19. Aświsanchālan / 135
20. Dandāsana / 135
21. Astānga Namaskār / 136
22. Bhujangāsana / 136
23. Parvatāsana / 137
24. Aświsanchālana / 137
25. Padhastāsana / 138
26. Hastotthānāsana / 138
27. Pranamasana / 139
28. Uttānpādāsana / 139
29. Pād Chakrāsana / 140
30. Pād Sanchālan / 140
31. Pawanmuktāsana / 141
32. Udarākarśan / 141
33. Pristha Sanchālan / 142
34. Chakki Chālāsana / 142
35. Naukachālāsana / 143
36. Kāsthatakśanāsana / 143
37. Tādāsana / 144
38. Tiryaktādāsana / 144
39. Katichakrāsana / 145
40. Siddhāsana / 145
41. Padmāsana / 146
42. Swastikasana / 146
43. Sukhāsana / 147
44. Paschimottānāsana / 147
45. Dhanurāsana / 148
46. Bhujangāsana / 148
47. Úalabhāsana / 149
48. Naukāsana / 149
49. Mārjariāsana / 150
50. Simhāsana / 150
51. Gomukhāsana / 151
52. Vipreet karnee āsana / 151
53. Sarvāngāsana / 152
54. Natrājāsana / 152
55. Śavāsana / 153
56. Nādiśodhan / 154
57. Bhrāmari / 155
58. Ujjai / 155
59. Sūryabhedan / 156
60. Bhastrikā / 156
61. Śītali / 157
62. Śītkāri / 157
63. Neti / 158
64. Dhauti / 159
65. Trātaka / 161
66. Nauli / 162
67. Savitā Dhyan / 164
68. So Ham Sadhana / 165
69. Yoga Nidra / 166
70. Yoga Nidrā / 169

Alphabetically

Ardhatitali / 129
Astānga Namaskār / 136
Aśwāsanchālan / 135
Aśwasanchālana / 137
Bhastri'kā / 156
Bhrāmari / 155
Bhujangāsana / 136
Bhujangāsana / 148
Chakki Chālāsana / 142
Dandāsana / 135
Dhanurāsana / 148
Dhauti / 159
Gomukhāsana / 151
Griva Sanchalan / 132
Gulf Ghūrnan / 127
Gulfnaman / 126
Hastotthānāsana / 134
Hastotthānāsana / 138
Initial Position / 125
Janu Chakra / 128
Janu Falak Akarsan / 128
Janunaman / 127
Kāsthatakśanāsana / 143
Katichakrāsana / 145
Kehuni Naman / 131
Manibandh Chakra / 131
Mārjariāsana / 150
Mustikabandh / 130
Nādiśodhan / 154
Natrājāsana / 152
Naukachālāsana / 143
Naukāsana / 149
Nauli / 162
Neti / 158
Pād Chakrāsana / 140
Pād Sanchālan / 140
Padanguli Naman / 126
Padhastāsana / 134
Padhastāsana / 138
Padmāsana / 146
Parvatāsana / 137
Paschimottānāsana / 147
Pawanmuktāsana / 141
Pranamasana / 133
Pranamasana / 139
Pristha Sanchālan / 142
Purnatitali / 129
Sarvāngāsana / 152
Śavāsana / 153
Savitā Dhyan / 164
Shronichakra / 130
Siddhāsana / 145
Simhāsana / 150
Śītali / 157
Śītkāri / 157
Skandhachakra / 132
So Ham Sadhana / 165
Sukhāsana / 147
Sūryabhedan / 156
Swastikasana / 146
Tādāsana / 144
Tiryaktādāsana / 144
Trātaka / 161
Úalabhāsana / 149
Udarākarśan / 141
Ujjai / 155
Uttānpādāsana / 139
Vipreet karnee āsana / 151
Yoga Nidra / 166
Yoga Nidrā / 169

Introduction

Yoga aims for the integrity of the body, mind, and spirit through a system of Asana, Pranayama and meditation. In reality, it consists of disciplines designed to bring humans closer to god. With the integration of the body, mind and spirit, you can attain a balance (physically and mentally) in your life as well as an inner peace to your body.

Yoga brings control over breathing and that works in effectively increasing the psycho-motor coordination. Practice of Yoga is a conscious process of gaining control over the mind, and thus concentration and attention-span improve, and hence intelligence of the children get increased.

In recent times there has been an increased awareness and interests in health and nature remedies. Yoga is an effective and time tested method for promoting and improving our health as well as prevention and management of diseases especially psychosomatic and degenerative chronic disorders. The scientific psycho-spiritual discipline of Yoga is the most precious gem of our culture and heritage and is being practiced in India for thousands of years.

Formerly, yoga was taught under the Gurukula system of ancient Indian Education pattern, but today it is gradually adopting modern methods of teaching and communication technologies. Recently, as the educationists become more and more aware about the lacune and short-comings or ills of modern education they have started looking hopefully towards yoga education as a useful complementary to overcome them. Modern yogis too appear to be favorably inclined to bring about a sort of integration between yoga and modern education. The only hitch is on "How to bring about such an integration of yoga into modern education with maximum advantages?" Firstly, modern educationists are convinced that yoga somehow can promote the aim of education. Secondly, scientific studies have shown that yoga can be helpful in promoting health and fitness. So yoga education can be usefully integrated with modern health education. Another point is, Educationists are increasingly becoming aware of the effective educational objectives in education. Yoga can also play a significant role in the effective education of students. Apart from that Yoga is found to provide strategies for successfully coping with various kinds of life stresses. This aspect can contribute much to the life-long education of students of all age-groups to confront stressful situation in life.

Lack of proper standardization of techniques and concepts of yoga is one of the stumbling blocks in the meaningful integration of yoga in education. Only increasing research, on this problem in particular, can bring about a better understanding amongst the institutions and teachers of yoga. Then it will be found easier and more effective for the proper integration of yoga in modern education.

There are no well-written, objectively presented, and relevant text-books for the use of students of different levels of their education. Text-books need to be written that can be useful, simple and objective, by collecting materials available from research studies carried out so far by different individuals and institutions of repute.

Yoga needs to be integrated in education rather as a boon to the students than as an additional burden. It is not necessary to add more and more yoga practices from lower to higher standards in schools, or colleges. selected yoga practices can be appropriated for the use of different types of learners to meet their specific requirements and problems. Coverage of syllabus need not be insisted. Instead, maximum contribution towards the welfare of the learners could be aimed at while selecting various items and contents from a sort of flexible syllabus.

Integration of Yoga into modern education calls for a research-oriented, objective approach than what has been attempted so far. Basically, yoga should be integrated in education to make it a source of relief and blessing to the students than an additional burden. Such integration should strive to present the depth and breadth of yoga science, its long history, vast literature; its impact on physical, mental, emotional and spiritual wellbeing of human beings – all presented objectively and insightfully.

Students are a valuable asset of any country or community as they are the future citizens. It is necessary to take care of their intelligence and well being. Scientist says that the students have many unexplained and unexpressed problems; they cannot express their problem correctly because of their growing age and hesitation. The advancement of the technology is coming into the new syllabus and it is coming with the information overload. Competitions, exams and tests not only manifest into academic anxiety and examofobia, they also manifest into regression and guilt.

Practice of Yoga not only helps to keep the mind strong and supple but also incorporate mental activities, and disciplines that help develop attention and concentration, and stimulate the creative ability that are latent within human body.

Several studies have been done in the field of Yoga and among them some have been based on children's well being and the effectiveness. Gharote, M.L. and Ganguly, S.K. (1975) have observed in their 3-week study on 430 school going children that selected practice of Yoga improves the muscular fitness of the 36.8% students of practice group.

Gharote, M.L (1976) again observed the effect of yogic practices on 44 children for three weeks and found a significant change in their physical health. Uma, K. et. al. (1989) observed the effect of Yogic practices on 45 children and found a significant change in IQ and Social Adaptation parameters in comparison to the non Yoga practitioner children after one year study.

Telles S. *et al.* (1993) observed the effect of yogic packages on 45 children in two groups and found a significant change in Attention span and Memory in the practice group after a ten days study. Baṭra, B.K., Nagratna, Dr. R. and Nagendra, Dr. H.R; (2003) observed in a study over 322 children that selected practice of Yoga improves analysing capacity. They also observed in their study over 300 children that selected practice of Yoga improves the memory of children.

Experts recommend few specific Asanas for them, as practice of Asana brings suppleness to the body and flexibility to the muscles and joints. But one should not only stop with asanas because asana without Pranayama is some times exhaustive. The practitioner may fall sick. Thus proper care should be taken and Pranayama should also be introduced especially for growing children, adolescent and college going students.

Practice of Prānāyamas not only brings harmony into both sympathetic and parasympathetic nervous system, but also improves the immunity and vital energy in the practitioners. Nādī śodhan, Bhastrikā, Śītalī, and Bhrāmari pranayamas should be practiced regularly in sequence of Yogic practices.

Meditation is one of the greatest resources for concentration memory and awareness. It is difficult to focus the mind at one point; so Gāyatri Mantra Japa is one of the best practices for meditation and concentration. Scientist says that the practice of meditation changes the way our brain works, and that thoughts can influence the brain and body. When his research team used MRI imaging to study the brains of four people meditating, they found increased activity in specific areas involved in attention and control of the autonomic nervous system.

Yoga instructor should make a package of every step of yoga including asana, pranayama and meditation so that the holistic development of the personality takes place among the practitioners, especially the students.

It is easy to practice and of course convenient to use audio tapes and television programmes to learn yoga but practice of yoga should not be done without the direct guidance of a Yoga expert. Yoga is a method of peeling off the subliminal sheath of conscious (external) mind that covers the inner core of the unconscious (inner) mind.

Yoga helps bring about subtle attitudinal change also in life, if taught earlier in life. If implemented in Schools, also it may bring a revolutionary change in the society. Harnessing ambition in a positive manner rather than through negativity will not only help the student excel but also make them a healthier and happier person for the country and the community.

Dr. Kamakhya Kumar

I

Introduction to Tradition of Yoga

YOGA: ITS MEANING AND IMPORTANCE

Yoga is the art of right living. It is based on the tenets of "simple living and high thinking." Yoga is a way of life, an integrated system of education for the body, mind and inner spirit. This art of right living was perfected and practiced in India thousands of years ago but, since Yoga deals with universal truth; its teachings are as valid today as they were in ancient times.

Practitioners of Yoga believe in a reality beyond the means of our senses (as the powers of these senses have limits, and thus they limit what we can know). What is currently beyond the means of my everyday perception is the concept of the Ultimate Reality, otherwise known as Atman/Brahman, Sat Chit Ananda–which is single and complete-I'd imagine that unity with this ultimate reality would be enlightenment and therefore our highest good- no more of the suffering of relative existence and boundless love, strength and compassion.

Many schools of Yoga believe that this state is utterly blissful. Thus Yoga is a practical aid, not a religion, and its techniques may be practiced by Buddhists, Jains, Christians, Muslims, Hindus, and atheists alike. Yoga is common for all.

Literally, the word Yoga means 'Union', the union of the finite with the infinite. The Word Yoga is derived from the Sanskrit root Yuj (To Join, to use, to concentrate one's attention on) meaning to bind, join, attach and Yoke to direct and concentrate one's attention on, to use and apply.

Etymologically the word 'Yoga' is derived from the Sanskrit root 'Yugira' meaning to write, to combine or to integrate. Gradually, the word Yoga gained three different meanings with different views.

Yugira yoge: Grammatically the word Yoga has been derived from the Sanskrit root Yugira. 'Yugira yoge' means union. The word Yoga has been used in this sense in Vedic sanhitas. The union of çhitta and soul is Yoga. This is the meaning of Yugira yoge.

Yuja samadhau: The word 'Yoga' derived from the Sanskrit root 'Yuja'— "Yuja-samadhau" stands for dhyana or Samadhi. While interpreting the word

Yoga in his commentary (bhasya) on various Upaniśads and the Gita Sankaraçharya Sankaraçharya considered the word Yoga as derivative of the root "yuj" meaning Samadhi.

Maharśi Vyasa in his commentary (bhasya) on patanjali's 'Yoga Sutra and Yagnavalkya on 'Sarva Darshan Sangraha' in the contept of patangali's Yoga Darshan interprete the word 'Yoga' as 'samadhi'.

Yuja sanyamane: Grammatically the word Yoga is used as the meaning "To control the senses".

Philosophically, the word 'Yoga' means union with the supreme spirit: what unites us with the supreme spirit is Yoga.

Technically, the word 'Yoga' has been used to refer to the system of philosophy propounded by Sage Patanjali about the second century B.C. but in general, Yoga may be called a method by which one can remove "ignorance", the cause of manifold, and thus attain union with the supreme self.

Yoga is a Sanskrit word which means union. From this root is derived the English word 'yoke'. The union implied here is an eternal truth. It is not something to be achieved by artifice, such as couples uniting in wedlock or nations uniting on the strength of peace treaties. Yoga signifies the essential unity that is the basis of life. In the highest sense, Yoga as spiritual union signifies the soul's union with the God.

Thus Yoga means "Union, balance, and a harmonious state of mind; bridging the different aspects of life; connecting the individual consciousness with the supreme consciousness; the union of the two—the lover and the beloved, the seeker and God, Śiva and Śakti, Ida and Pingla, the sun and the moon, active and passive."

Maharśi Patanjali defined Yoga as:

Yogasçhitta vritti nirodhah

—Patanjal Yoga Sutra 1/2

Meaning: Yoga is restraining the mind-stuff (çhitta) from taking various forms (*vrittis*). Yoga is the science by which we stop çhitta from assuming, or becoming transformed into, several faculties.

As the reflection of the moon on the sea is broken or blurred by the waves, so is the reflection of the Atman the true self, broken by the mental waves. Only when the sea is stilled to mirror like calmness can the reflection of the moon be seen, and only when the 'Mind stuff', the *çhitta*, is controlled to absolute calmness, is the self to be recognized. According to Kath Upaniśad:

// Yadā pancāvatisthante Inānani manasa Saha, budhis/
/ ca na Vicestati, tam ahuh pa ramān gatim //
// Tam Yogam-iti-manyante sthiram-indriya dhāranām/

/apramattas-tadā bhavati, Yoga-hi prabhavāpyayau //

—Kath Upaniśad, 3.3.10-11

Meaning: The highest state is that, when the five senses of knowledge, together with the manas (the lower mental faculty) cease from their normal activities and the buddhi (pure intellect) it self doesn't stir. They consider being the state of Yoga, the firm holding back of the senses, when one is completely undistracted. Yoga, verily, is the beginning and end (birth and death).

The Yoga Vaśistha defines Yoga as a device that makes one reach the other shore of the stream of sorrow. It is indeed true that a yogi is a person who is eternally free of cravings and sorrows. He overcomes ignorance for good or forever.

Maharśi Aurobindo says the meaning of the word Yoga is to join our eternal consciousness with our true self—the divine within ourselves; which is one every where.

We find Yoga defined at different places in the Gita. The first is Yoga is equanimity in success and failure. The second is Yoga is skill and efficiency in action. The third is Yoga is the supreme secret of life. The next one is Yoga is the giver of untold happiness. The next one is Yoga is serenity. And then Yoga is the destroyer of pain. There are many more definitions in Gita only.

Yogasthah Kuru Karmāni Sangam Tyaktwā Dhananjaya /
Sidyaśidhyosamobhuktwā Samatwam Yoga Uçhyate //

Meaning: O, Arjuna perform your duties well, established in the Yogic way of life, without any attachment. Treat success and failure alike, such equanimity is called Yoga.

// Buddhiyukto Jahātiha Ubhe Sukritaduskrite /
TasmādYogāy Yujyaswa Yogah Karmaśu Kauśalam //

Meaning: Endowed with this evenness of mind, one frees oneself in this life, alike from vice and virtue; devote yourself therefore, to this Yoga. Yoga is the very dexterity of work. It is skill and effectiveness in action.

// Tam VidyaddukhasanyogviYogam Yogasangyitam //

Meaning: That state which is free from the contact of sorrow, is called Yoga.

Yoga, through repeated experiments throughout its history of more than 5,000 years, established that consciousness is the most fundamental essence of creation at macrocosmic as well as microcosmic level. This viewpoint has been formed not through pronouncements of a single individual but is the result of profound investigation by a number of seers and sages of the Vedas, independently through *tapas* since aeons. What they did through their *tapas* was not only introspection, but by diving deep within themselves saw that everything tangible was explicable in terms of consciousness. This consciousness pervaded not only in their psychic being but also in their vitality, physicality and also the entire cosmos, and each manifestation pervaded by it.

Introspection is only an outer façade of their approach, just a beginning. Mind for them is a tool of understanding and whatever dawned before the introspecting mind could not be sheer physical. The seer turned his consciousness within with the result that he was able to reach the root of consciousness lying in his self-transcendence. On reaching that state, he found out consciousness as all in all in transcendence as well as in immanence. In transcendence it remained in its pure form and in immanence it assumed all possible forms the world consists of. Thus, while the *purusa* of Patanjali and that of introspecting psychologists remained confined to his individual being as totally exclusive of the universal, the Vedic seer rose in transcendence beyond the universal. He realized in him the individual and the universal as two phases of the transcendent with which he came to identify himself by virtue of his sharing in the transcendent consciousness.

This is also evident from multitude seers who produced huge archetypal ideas, myths, legends and principles that are common with less possibility of mutual give and take in most of the cases. This uniformity in their experience has no explanation except for the commonness of the psychic ground happening so large in number and with so many spans of time amongst them in terms of both space and time. On analysis of Jung's Theory of Archetypes, one finds that it is quite possible for people belonging to different nationalities and ages to produce similar archetypal images but in no case quite identical. The similarity in such cases is due to inherence of the collective unconscious in common within the whole mankind, the dissimilarity is due to the possibility of variations in the composition of that unconscious itself, as it is formed out of varying experiences of mankind throughout the globe right from its animal ancestry.

This was the one of the extraordinary event in the history of mankind since it involved so much absorption on the part of the aspirant of knowledge so as to become completely coincident to the very object of knowledge. In fact, we cannot deny that the more deeply we get ourselves involved in intricacies of the composition of an object, the better we understand it. It is only through such an involvement with the area of research that scientists have come to understand so much of life and the world at the physical level. Now at the end of their investigation from this standpoint, they are beginning to realize the extent to which consciousness contributes in determining the shape of things not only on the commonsense but also on the scientific. This is evident from the fact that when a scientist starts his investigation into the shape of the ultimate constituent of matter with the presupposition that it may be something like a particle, it appears to him like that and when he starts the same with the probability of it being wave-likes; it appears exactly before him. This experimentation on the scientific level bears not only the supremacy of consciousness vis-à-vis matter but also its creativity in shaping its notion of the physical.

When we ponder over the creative capability of consciousness as working within us, we find it hard to resist the conclusion that this capability must have its source in the corresponding creativity of consciousness in its pure form. It this creativity of consciousness can handle and mould matter anyway it chooses, as we learn from the experiments of scientists, we are left with no option but affirm that consciousness must have come to have evolved these capabilities on the human level by virtue of being the real source of matter. This is what the Vedic seers contend through their admission of the origin of the physical in pure consciousness as Atman and Brahman present in their concentricity and extensity. Thus organic and inorganic are only manifestation of consciousness which is both transcendent and immanent.

The importance of yoga is in its amenability to render the entire content of the human psychology in terms of consciousness. No doubt scriptures produced world over have contributed to the moderation of human psychology so as to check its inherent violent nature throughout the ages. If there had not been check of this nature in the form of scriptural prescriptions, man would have left the world in havoc. Today man is faced with the practical utilities of science which has negated the utility, appeal and value of these scriptures. In this process of evaluation, modern psychology has played an important role. Physical science abstained itself from entering into the domain of spirituality had not psychology attacked the inherent consciousness and sided with physical sciences exclusively to explain the phenomenon of consciousness as a by-product of the physical like the Carvakas. Man finding himself defenseless took resort to faith and declared it as inviolable but this inviolability has also been shaken and sooner or later it, has give way to a thorough analysis for its tenability. In this exercise, faith does not seem to have any bright future on account of its sheer non-rationality.

Herein lies the advantage of Vedic yoga since its entire structure is based on consciousness as the basic stuff of creation in all its forms and varieties. Vedic seers by means of deep meditation were able to see through everything, howsoever gross and mightily tangible it may be, as a formation of consciousness. This has been the finding of not one or two seers, but of many seers, living over a million square kilometer of the Indian soil for thousands of years in isolated groups sequestered from one another by considerable distance hurdled with rivers, forests and wild animals, etc. Despite all the distractions, their common concurrence on consciousness as the essential stuff of creation is astounding and much more than the modern physicist's discovery regarding convertibility of matter into energy. While the physicist's discovery boosted the effort of the psychologist to create a psychology with matter as its basic stuff, the Vedic seers left the entire legacy of consciousness as the same sort of stuff to think of the possibility of formulating a psychology of the psyche.

When we study the present situation, we find that the modern psychology reigning between the tension of opposites, namely the real and the ideal. The real is our past animal nature, pulling us back to itself in the form of instinctive drives while the ideal is our effort to make adjustment in the mode of fulfillment of our instinctive drives so as to conform to the social norms of the day. The animal nature is self-seeking while the ideal conforms to the social norms, requiring moving beyond sheer self-interest so as to concede to the requirements of others involved in the given situation, be they members of family, neighbours, classmates, colleagues, or any sort of people who have an interest to be shared with. It is only around this point that the modern psychology is moving under different denominations, behavioural, transactional, industrial, educational, marital, psychoanalytical, to name just a few. The interaction of the opposites creates tension while the psychologist is seeking to remove the same through adjustments and readjustments. The adjustments and readjustments are tried upon under the presumption that both the real and the ideal have a common origin—the physical. Thus, a modern psychologist removes, sets and resets psychological factors as per requirements of given situations and he has nothing to think about beyond this adjustments and readjustments. On account of having adopted the norm of physical sciences, the modern psychology envisages the human life as a machine to be kept on working properly unmindful of any aim or objective before it in any sense. If a living being, particularly a human begin to be treated as a machine, how can it be expected to have an objective of its own apart from its amenability to exploitation by its owner?

If the human conscience is left with anything alive in it that seeks fulfillment, it can be fulfilled through Vedic yoga and can have the joy of that fulfillment in abundance without turning anywhere else. This is due to its basic postulate of consciousness as the source and essence of everything. According to it even the instinctive life can be explained in terms of consciousness as its source and basis. Explanation for it is to be found in concentricity of consciousness, i.e. consciousness in the form of individual consciousness. It needs to be understood that consciousness is prone as much to concentricity as to extensity.

As the individual consciousness is identical with the entire cosmos and as all entities arise from him, and because of the knowledge of all the subjects, he has the feeling of identity with them all, hence whether in word, object or thought, there is no state which is not Consciousness. In fact, the experiment himself is always and everywhere abides in the form of the experienced i.e.

Consciousness, which is the essential Experiment and abides in the form of the cosmos as its field of experience. This is so because the experiment constitutes the entire cosmos, and therefore, there is no state whether it is the beginning or the middle or the end and whether it is word, or object or ideation which is not Consciousness.

The methods of Yoga can be pursued without recourse to any dogma, and they require the same rigor as science insists, namely, observation, experimentation, and verification by repeatable experience. Yoga can be looked upon as the experiential basis for philosophical speculations and conclusions, and if rightly used, Yoga can be a bridge between philosophy and science.

Yoga claims that it has developed methods, which can deal with the supra-physical as rigorously and as objectively as modern science deals with physical phenomena. Yoga claims that its methods can deal both with the physical and supra-physical, and, if needed and encouraged it could develop an integral science of both the physical and supra-physical and their interrelationship.

HISTORY OF YOGA

The origin of Yoga is obscured in its great antiquity. Historically what we know about it is very little. Undoubtedly, it is a gigantic task to understand the systematic development and various progressive stages of the development of Yoga.

It is beyond doubt that all the saints and sages (seers) of Aryavarta have been practicing Yoga since time immemorial. Moreover, it is a well known fact that Lord *Brahma* is the creator of the universe and that he had to perform austerity (*Tapa*) to create this universe. This austerity (Penance) performed by lord Brahma is nothing else but an integral part of Yoga itself. Highlighting the divine tradition of Yoga in the form of austerity Goswami Tulsidasji writes:

// Tapa Ādḥār Sab Sṛsti Bḥavānī //

—Balkānda, Rāmçharitmānas

Meaning: In fact, the entire creation, Bhawani rests on penance. He again highlights the divine tradition of Yoga when he writes:

// Mātu Pitahi Bahu Vidḥi Samujḥāyī/
Çhalī Umā Tapa Hita Harśāyī//

—Balkānda, Rāmçharitmānas

Then, after consoling her parents in every possible way, Uma gladly went away to practice penance. Thus we find that Yoga was practiced not only by saints and sages but also by God and Goddess. And, under such conditions it is very difficult to say when the divine tradition of Yoga began. If we admit the fact that Lord Brahma succeeded in creating the universe by the power of penance we will have to admit that the Yoga is as old as the universe itself.

According to mythical tradition, Śiva is said to be the founder of Yoga and Parvati is his first disciple. Lord Śiva represents supreme consciousness and Parvati represents supreme knowledge, will and action, and is responsible for all creation. Parvati is regarded as the Mother of the whole universe. The individual soul is embodied and bound to the world of name and form, and also liberated from the bondage of the world and united with supreme consciousness through her grace. Out of Love and compassion for her children, she imparted her secret knowledge of liberation in the form of Tantra. The techniques of Yoga have their source in Tantra and the two can't be separated, just as consciousness *(Śiva),* can't be separated from energy *(Śakti).*

Lord Śiva himself developed the system of Yoga. In different ages and different periods of history, Ṛśis, sages and saints propounded and expounded it.

The first books to refer to Yoga were the ancient 'Tantras' and later the 'Vedas' which were written about the time when the Indus Valley culture was flourishing. Although they don't give specific practices, they reflect Yoga symbolically. In fact, the verses of the Vedas were heard by the ṛśis, seers, in states of deep, yogic meditation or Samadhi, and are regarded as revealed scriptures. It is however in the Upaniśads that Yoga began to take a more definable shape. These scriptures collectively form Vedanta, the culmination of the Vedas and are said to contain the essence of the Vedas.

Yoga has been defined and explained by many yogis, saints, scholars and philosophers but it is to maharśi *Pātanjali* that credit goes for systematizing it. When deities and demons had churned the ocean, they used the mountain Sumeru as the churning rod in the process. From that churning, nectar came out and lord Viśnu kept it in a jar. Likewise, Yoga (the nectar or Brahma vidya) was kept by Maharśi *Pātanjali* in a jar which we know as the Yoga-Sutra of Patanjali.

In the *Purānas* (Indian Spiritual Scriptures) we can read the story of Patanjali's birth. His mother, Gonika, was an unmarried tapasvini (Lady Practitioner of Yoga). Having gained tremendous knowledge and great wisdom and not finding any right disciple to whom she could transfer her knowledge, she prayed to the Sun God and as an oblation took water in her hand, saying, 'this knowledge has come through you, so let me give it back to you' At that moment she opened her eyes and saw something move in her hand. This was Patanjali '*pata*' means fallen; '*anjali*' stands for ' the time of prayer'. Thus the name Patanjali was given to him by his mother, according to the manner of his birth.

It was he who wrote the Mahabhasya, the great treatise on grammar. He also learned dance and through dance movements he came to know the various functions of the body and so he wrote a treatise on health and medicine. When he had written these two treatises, he felt that his work was still incomplete, as he had not touched consciousness. So he said to himself, ' Now let me speak of consciousness', and he began to write his **Yoga Sutras**.

It is true that credit goes to Patanjali for systematizing Yoga but even then the question "who was the first speaker of Yoga", remains unanswered, as in the first aphorism maharśi Patanjali writes:

Atḥa Ỵogāṇuśāsanam

—Patanjali Yoga Sutra 1/1

Meaning: Now there fore, complete instructions regarding Yoga. Maharśi Patanjali could have used *Atha yogānuśāsanam,* which means, 'here are instructions on Yoga,' but he used the word *atha*. '*Atha*' means ' now there fore,' which means that these instruction on Yoga are in connection with some previous instructions.

This proves that maharśi patanjali is not the first speaker of Yoga but he has only written **Yoga sutra**. Who is the first speaker of Yoga? In this regard it would be relevant to quote the opinions of some saints. Maharśi *Yāgavalkya* is of the opinion that:

Hiraṇyagarbḥo Yogaṣya Vaktā nāṇyah pụrātanah

—Yoga Yāgyavalkya

The first speaker of Yoga is Aḉharya *Hiranyagarbha*; the name is as old as **He** is. Even Maharśi Vyaśa states that:

Sānḳḥyaṣya Vaktā Kapilah Parmarśih Sā Uḉḥyate.
Hiraṇyagarbho Yogaṣya Vaḳtā Nāṇyah Purātanah.

—Mahābhārat

Meaning: The speaker of Samkhya Philosophy is the great seer Kapila and the speaker of the Yoga Philosophy is Hiranyagarbha. No other speakers of Yoga are as old as Hiranyagarbha.

Now the question arises who is this *Hiranyagrbha*, there are seven *Hiranyagarbha* but who is the speaker of Yoga? For example the sun is regarded as the first Hiranyagarbha. The second one is *Mahat Tattva* or *Budhi.* We have the resumption of the third *Hiranyagarbha* as a great yogi in '*Ahirbahdhnusanhita*'.

The fourth *Hiranyagarbha* described in ' *Yogaśikhopaniśad*' has been regarded as the devotee and disciple of lord Śiva. The fifth Hiranyagarbha named Uttama is famous as the father of *Urja ṛśi*. The sears of Vedic period are known as the sixth Hiranyagarbha. The seventh *Hiranyagarbha* is regarded as ḉhaturmukha Brahma. Even the Veda States:

Hiraṇyagarḅhah Samvarṭatāgre
Bhūtaṣya gyātah patireka Āsit
Sadādhana Pṛthivion Dḥamuteman
Kasonai Devāya Haviśā Vidḥem.

—Ṛg Veda 10.12.1

However it is very difficult to decide who the first speaker of Yoga is. Some scholars are of the opinion that actually Hiranyagarbha was the form of Brahma. Chattergi S.K. Atreya writes in Indian culture that Hiranyagarbha is the first expounder of Yoga. On the other hand Lord Kṛśna in the Holy Gita says:

Imān vivaṣṿate Yogam pṛokṭavānahamavyayam/
Vivaṣvanone nave pṛaha Manuṛkṣṿakave' bṛavīt/
Evam paramparapṛaptamionam ragar
sayo viduh sa kaleneha mahate Yoga

—Srīmadbhagvad Gīta 4/1-2

Meaning: I taught this immortal Yoga to Vivasvan (Sun-God; Vivasvan conveyed it to Manu (his son); and Manu imparted it to (his son) *Ikśvāku*. Thus transmitted successfully from father to son, Arjuna, this Yoga remained known to the Parijarsis (royal sages). It has, ever, long since disappeared from this earth. He further says:

Sā evayam Māyā te'dya Yogah proktāh purātanah/
Bhakto'si me sakhā çeti rahasyam hyetaduttamam//

—Śrīmadbhagvad Gīta

The same ancient Yoga has this day been imparted to you by me, because you are my devotee and friend; and also because this is a supreme secret. In order to take a brief survey of the historical development of Yoga based on the available sources and yogic literature we may consider the different periods of history in next chapter.

The beginning of the Yoga tradition are undoubtedly shrouded in the mists of antiquity, but it is universally recognized that Indian Yoga constitutes one of the oldest and most important scientific spiritual legacies of humanity and has been preached as well as practiced uninterruptedly since the dawn of humans history.

Pre-Vedic Period

The excavation of seals portraying deities in stone-honoured meditative postures in the sites at Mohanjodaro and Harappa of the Indus Valley period

(3000-2000 BC) strongly suggests that the Yoga tradition is fact given special recognition in the Indian society well before the Vedic period.

The idol of mother Goddess and the figure seated in the yogic posture suggests the actuality of Yoga. Some believe that Yoga owes much to the Pre-Aryan heritage.

Vedic Period

Although scholars differ in their opinion about the connection of Indus Valley Civilization with Vedic Civilization, the source of Yoga is undoubtedly found in the Vedic Literature.

Some scholars are of the opinion that the divine tradition of Yoga begin with the very resonance of *Vedic Ṛçhās* (Vedic Mantras) in the caves of *Devātmā Himālayas*. With the very first ray of civilization the divine light of Yoga spread in human life. The essence of the divine knowledge of the ancient seers lies in this very Yaga.

We have the description of the importance of Yoga in Srutis (the essence of Vedas known through aural transmission), Smritis and Puraṇas.

Even the *Ṛgveda,* which is the oldest book in the world, speaks of Mantras regarding yogic practices. Mantras like 10/177/1 of the Ṛg-Veda and 10/2/30-32/8/83 of the Atharva Veda bears testimony to this fact.

We have the description of different processes of Yoga in *Āitreya Aranyaka 2/17,3/1,3/4,3/6, Taitteriya Aranyaka-2/2, 2/7, 2/9, Śatpath Brahmana 1/4/4/7, 14/3/2/3, Taittiriya brahonana-3/10/18/6, 1/2/6.* On the other we find the growth of certain yogic tenets in the Brahmanas like Kayusitaki, Jaiminiya and Gopath. In these we get elaborate description of Pranavidya and advance ideas regarding Pranavidya. Pranava is another technical name for Om.

Upaniśadic Period

There are several Upaniśads like, Kena, Katha, Kausitakl, Prasna, Mundaka, Mandukya, Taittiriya, Aitareya, chandoga, Brahadaranyaka and Svetasvatara etc reflect Yoga in some forms or the other.

Anyone who reads them in the original Sanskṛt is caught up and carried away by the elevation, profundity and compelling fascination of the pregnant, often poetic utterances through which they unravel the mysterious and sacred relations of the human soul with the ultimate reality. Arthur Schopenhaver was among the leading German philosophers of the last centuries who got acquainted with some early Upaniśads through a Latin rendering from a person translation. He was so impressed and moved by what he read in them that he wrote the following inspiring and oft-quoted words—an English translation of his German outpouring:

"From every sentence, deep, original and sublime thoughts arise and the whole is pervaded by a high and holy and end earnest spirit..." In the whole world there is no study, except that of the originals, so beneficial and as elevating as that of the Upaniśads. It has been the solace of any life; it will be the solace of my death".

Upaniśads like *Ḉḥhandogya and Bṛhadaranyaka* which reflects the basis of *KṛyāYoga, Prāna and Nādis* are important topics discussed here. In *Kathopanidśad* the word Yoga has been used in its technical sense, whereas in upaniśads like *Iśa, Kena and Katha* we have the information of the firm basis of Yoga.

In fact *Śvetāsvatar Upaniśad* is regarded as the most authentic book on Yoga vidya as it describes the essence of yogic practices and their physiological effects. Upaniśads like *Aitareya* and *Taittṛya* reflects different Kos'as of the body.

Epic Period

We have the description of Yoga even in great Indian epics like Ramayana and Mahabharata. These epics are the rich source of information about various kinds of yogic practices. *Goswāmi Tulsidās* writes:

Viśwamiṭṛa Mahāmuni Ḡyāni /
Basahin Bipin samu Aśram Jāni //
Jahān Japa Jagya Joga Muni Karahin /

—Balkanda Ramayana

Meaning: The great enlightened sage Viśvamitra lived in a forest, during it a sacred retreat. There he practiced Japa (continuous repetition or Muttering of sacred-formulas) and Yoga (contemplation) and performed sacrifices.

Thus Yoga seems to be quite popular in the age of Ramayana. Even Maharśi Valmiki used to perform Yoga. He also used to make Lava and Kusa practice Yoga in his hermitage.

The most important section dealing with Yoga in mahabharata is the famous Bhagawad Gita. The Gita in fact is an ocean of Yoga. It is a store house of Yogas like Jnana, Karma and Bhakti. While highlighting the importance of Yoga, Lord Kṛśna says to Arjuna:

// Tapaṣvibhyo' dhiko yogi Ḡyānibḥyo'pi mato dḥikah
karmibḥyascādhiko yogi tasmād yogi bhavārjunaḥ//

—Śrīmadbhagvad Gīta 6/46

Meaning: The yogi is superior to the ascetics; he is regarded as superior even to those verses in sacred lore. The yogi is also superior to those who

> perform action with some interested motive. There fore, be thou a yogi, o Arjuna.

The Bhagvad Gita, which forms part of the 'Mahabharata' epic is considered by many to have been composed by Vyasa before 50 BC, refers to the Yoga tradition as puratana (Meaning—'ancient' or 'age-obi') in the oft-quoted third verse of chapter four.

Thus the internal evidence of many ancient Sanskṛt classics also suggests that Yoga constitutes a very, very old tradition and was considered 'ancient' well before the commencement of the present Christian era.

Whatever uncertainties there may be in establishing the actual date in the distant past of the beginnings of this unique science of man in depth and spirituality of sell-unfoldment rests, surely and securely, on the triune bedrock of the early Upaniśads, the Yoga sutras and the Bhagavad-Gita.

The Bhagvad-Gita is, indeed, pregnant with all types of Yoga. Jnana Yoga, Karma Yoga and Bhakti Yoga are sweet fruits of the Bhagvad Gita.

Eoneritus, a very senior professor at Princeton, USA, reading a French translation of the Bhagvad-Gita, wrote:

> The beauty of the poem affected me instantly, from the very first line. As for the thought that inspired it, I felt, I found in it the only form of religious thought that could satisfy my mind.

The American philosopher Henry Thoreau felt so stimulated and enlightened by the Gita that he gave expression to his deep sense of admiration and gratitude to this scripture in the following oft-quoted words:

> "In the morning I bathe my intellect in the stupendous and cosmogonal philosophy of modern world and its literature seem puny and trivial".

Mahatma Gandhi was deeply influenced by the Gita and writes these memorable words.

> "When doubts haunt me, when disappointments stare me in the face and I see not one ray of hope on the horizon, I turn to the Bhagvad Gita and find a verse here and a line there to comfort me, and I immediately begin to smile in the midst of over whelming sorrow... . Those who meditate on The Gita will derive fresh joy and new meanings from it every day."

The 11th and 12th verses of 6th chapter in the Gita tell us how lord Kṛśna orders us to practice Yoga:

/ *Śuçhau Deśe Pratiṣṭhāpya Sṭhirmāsanmātmanah* /
/ *Nātyuçhçhhitam Nāatinīçham Çhailājinakuśottaram* //
/ *Tatṛaikagṛam Manah Kṛitwa Yatçhittendṛyakṛyaḥ* /
/ *Upaviśyāsane YunjyādYogamātmviśuḍdhaye* //

—Śrīmadbhagvad Gīta 6/11-12

Meaning: having firmly placed his seat in a spot which is free from dirt and other impurities with the sacred kusa grass, a deerskin and a cloth spread there on one below another (Kusa below, deerskin in the middle and cloth uppermost), neither very high nor very Low.

And occupying that seat, concentrating the mind and controlling the functions of the mind and senses, he should practice Yoga for self-purification.

Sutra Period

As well understood and appreciated by serious students of Yoga, the Yoga-sutras consist of just 196 short statements or aphorism (sutras), divided into four sections entitled Samadhi (unitive experience), *sādhanā* (spiritual practice), vibhuti (para-normal attainments), According to tradition, this work was composed by *Pātamjali,* whose date is uncertain, but is believed in to have lived around 300 B.C.

Thus Patanjali's Yoga Sutras are the oldest, systematic treatise on Yoga available to us. It is based on the previous and contemporary traditions of Yoga. Several commentaries have been written on the Yoga sutras of Patanjali which throw light on the development of different yogic concepts and techniques of that period. The first commentary on Yoga sutras is known as *Vyāsabhāsya.*

As we are aware, the first authentic English translation of the Yoga-Sutra as along with a detailed commentary, also in English, was made by I.K. Taimni a professor of chemistry at Allahabad University. He Looked upon Yoga as the science of sciences and has the following to say in his introduction to this book:

> "It stands in its own right as a science based upon the eternal Laws of the higher life and doesn't require the support of any science or philosophical system to uphold its claims. Its truths are based on the experiences of mystics, Occultists, Saints and sages who have realized and borne witness to then throughout the ages...."

Buddhist Period

Gautam Budha (563-483 BC) is perhaps the first important historical figure of the Yoga tradition, whose date can be fixed, whose life can be sketched and whose teachinos on the problems of human existence and destiny can be ascertained with some measure of certainty. It is reasonably obvious, however that the meditative practices associated with the advanced stages of yogic discipline were well established in India long before lord Buddha was born.

We have a very clear description of Yoga in the fundamental principles of Buddhism. We have the description of Astanga Yoga or eight fold path of Yoga in "***Dharma çhakra pravartan sutra***".

Lord Buddha himself had practiced Yoga under the teachers Arada kalam and uddaka Ramaputta. There are striking similarities of concepts and terms in early Buddhist scriptures and Yoga sutras of Patanjali.

The four folds dhyanas referred to by early Buddhist scriptures is one of the significant contributions to Yoga. Besides the four fold dhyanas in Buddhist texts are described the four Brahona vihras of sublime occupations cultivating four exalted psychological moods which are:

(1) Love (*Maitṛ*) (2) Compassion *(Karunā)*
(3) cheerfulness *(Muditā)*, and (4) Indifference *(Upekśā)*.

Following are the some remarkable resemblances between Patanjali Yoga system and early Buddhist Yoga: Both accept the four noble truths and emphasize that Yoga removes misery.

Both don't consider the absolute necessity of God as head. Buddha is silent while according to Patajali it is one of the alternative paths. Both accept the concept of Samadhi.

There is ideological and terminological similarly between Nirvana and Samadhi. There is a parallelism in using eight fold path of Yoga.

Jainism Period

We have the description of five Yamas as 'Anuvrata' in Jainism. Lord Mahavira himself was a great yogi. We have a very clear description of Patanjal Yoga in book like 'Yogabindu' written by Haribhadra Suri and 'Adhyatmasar ' by Yaśovijay. Mahavira, the founder of Jainism was a contemporary of Gautam Buddha and was undoubtedly a great practical yogi.

Yoga according to Jain tradition also consists in yoking body, speech, and mind. It is called Upa Yoga. Jains speak of the three folds Yoga-Jnana Yoga, Isçha Yoga and Kṛya Yoga. Much of the Jain teachings resemble those of the Bhagvad Gita.

Jainism accepts right outlook and right-knowledge to gather as the path of liberation. In the Jain religion both devotion and meditation find a place. Some Jain texts, like the Yoga Sastra of Hemacandha, mentions several asanas or postures which are identical with those of Tantra and Yoga.

In Subhadra's Jnanarnava (500AD), there are several chapters on Yoga as well as long discussions on Asana, Pranayama, Mandala, Dharana and Dhyana. Other texts give instructions on Nyasa, the technique from which Yoga nidra evolved.

It is obvious that Jainism has been influenced by tantra. In the **Tattvartha-sara-dipika**, a Jain scripture of the fifteenth century, there are various techniques for awakening Kundalini and the pranic centers in the body aspirants are instructed to imagine lotus flowers where the çharkas are situated and to visualize them with different numbers of petals, each inscribed with a letter or mystical syllable. These letters are mantras and the practitioner is instructed to repeat the mantra which corresponds to the lotus he is visualizing.

Meditation resulting in liberation in Jainism said to be fourfold: Righteous meditation, auspicious meditation, white meditation, and pure meditation.

The available works on Jainism are of post Patanjali period. There are several later works by Jain authors dealing with different types and aspects of Yoga written under the influence of Patanjali's Yoga Sutra and Hath Yoga.

Some of the important ones may be mentioned as 'Yoga-sastra' by Hem Çhandra with his own commentary on it, Yogabindu, Pravaçhan Sara, Yoga Drstimasutra, Uttara Dhyayana ete.

Smṛti Period

The period of smṛti literature starts from the times of Patanjali, some Smṛties had been composed before 500 BC and they were written till about 1000 A.D. During this long period of smṛti literature, we find the changes in the Traveling Ideas, beliefs, worships, and customs. The Smṛties tried to combine Yoga with the daily rituals. Thus we find Pranayama and certain purificatory techniques occupying important place in every ritual.

We have the description of non-violence, truth, non-stealing, cleanliness in the following verses:

//Ahinsāsạtyamāsteyam śawçḥmindṛya nigṛaha etam samasikam Dḥarma /
Çḥatuṛvaerma bṛavibmanu//

—Manusmṛti 10/63

Again we have the description of pranayama in the following verse of the Manusmṛti:

Dahante dḥỵāyamananām-Dhatunām yatha malaha/
Tathendṛyānām Dahante Dośāh pranasya nigrahata//

Meaning: Just as all the dirt of the metals are removed by fire, Likewise pranayama removes all the dirt of the *Yagnavalkyc smṛṭti 4/64* states that: The aspirant should practice hundred pranayama to kill all types of sins.

Pauranic Stage

We have the description of yogic kriyas at several places in puranas. The orthodox number of Puranas is 18. Puranas like Śiva, Vayu, Brahmanda, steanda etc are mostly led with the description of yogic kriyas. Even Śrīmad Bhagvad Purana is pregnant with Yoga. Many of these Puranas deal with Yogasanas. We have the description of Yama and Niyama in the following verses of Viśnupurana:

Brahmaçhryamahinsām çha satyasteyaparigrahān sevent yogi
Niskamo yogyatam svam mano nayan/
Svādhyāya śauçhasantośatpansi Niyatatmavana.
Kurvita Brahmani tatha parsimanpravanam Manah//
—Viśnupurana, 6/7/36-38]

We have the description of few Asanas like Swastikasana in Śrīmad Bhagvad Purana. Puranas speak of two types of Pranayama. They are Agarbha and Sagarbha. ***Agarbha***-Pranayama performed in accordance with ratio without japa and dhyana. ***Sagarbha***-Pranayama performed with japa and dhyana. Sagarbha is considered to be the best pranayama.

We have the description of these Pranayamas in the following verses of the Śivapurana:

Agarbhaśçha Sagarbhaśçha Prānayāmo didha şmŗtāha/
japa dhyānabinagarbhah sagarbhastat smanvayāt//.
Agarbhada garbha sanyuktah Prānayāmaha Śatedhikaha/
Tasmāt sayarbha kurvanti yoginaha Pramasan yamama//
—Śiva purana, uttarkhanda, 33-34

Medieval Period (Tantra Stage)

There is a vast literature on Tantras published and unpublished. There are Buddhist Tantras, Hindu Tantras and Jain Tantras. Tantras commonly deal with śakti-worship, mudras, mantras, Mandalas, the five Makaras, the Dakśinamarga, vama-marga, and magic practices for acquiring supernatural powers. Seventh to twelfth century was the period of tantrik works and cults, both Hindu and Bhudhist.

The tantriks substituted Yoga of enjoyment for the Yoga of abstinence and asceticism. The tantras claim that liberation is achieved by the very means by which otherwise one falls. the tantras tried to differentiate three dispositions of animal disposition which are graded according to the nature and stage of the practicants. It is in the final disposition that the practicant rises above sense enjoyment altogether.

Natha Cult: As an aid to Raja Yoga Hatha Yoga was evolved and became very popular through the Natha cult. Many of the hathayogic practices seem to have their origin in Tantrism. NathaYoga laid a great emphasis on preparing the body as a vehicle for attaining the higher spiritual experiences. It is this Yoga which has become popular throughout the world. Some of important and traditional texts are: 'Siddha-Sidhanta Paddhati', 'Goraksa Sataka', 'Hatha Pradipika', 'Gheranda Samhita', Siva Sanhita'.

Bhakti Cult: Yoga also had its impacts on Bhakti literature. The Bhagvada Purana is looked upon as a Bible by the vaisnavita sect. The sandilya sutras and Narada sutras deal systematically with different aspects of Bhakti.

Modern Period

The divine tradition of Yoga continues even today without any break. It is ever flowing like the Ganga. In modern times swami Vivekananda made Yoga popular. Swami Ramtirtha and Paramhansa Yogananda continued their work to spread the divine knowledge of Yoga out of India.

The Great yogis like Śrī Ramkṛshna Paramhamsa, Pt. Śrī Ramsharma Acharya, Raman Maharśi, Maharśi Aurobindo, Adisankarachya, etc. of the recent past are some of the glorifying examples of spiritual transformation.

The west came in contact with Yoga during the times of Plato and Aristotle who paid rich tributes to Indian philosophy in their works. These contacts were furthered with the Indian conquests of Alexander in the third century BC. Westerners who came to know about Yoga were more interested in mysticism. The formation of Asiatic Society of Bengal gave further fillip to Yoga. The society concentrated on studying all the culture and mysticism associated with India. Their research and translations included essays on the Vedas, Yoga, and the poetry of Śankara. Many of the Indian epics and Vedas were translated into English. Bhagvat Gita was one of such translations. In the early 19th century, Yoga was introduced to the western world through translated works.

Modern Yoga arrived in the United States during the late 1800's. It can be attributed to many gurus, including Swami Vivekananda, and their apostolic works. The Germans also discovered the beauty of the Sanskrit language and Vedic mystery. Max Muller was the pioneer among the German scholars who contributed immensely to the popularity of Indian culture and mysticism. In the late 1800's and early 1900's, Yoga masters began to travel to the west, attracting attention and followers. Hatha Yoga was the most popular Yoga form in the west. Slowly and gradually Yoga came to assume importance in matters related to health, peace, fitness and spirituality.

Some research institutes like Bihar School of Yoga, Munger, Swami Vivekananda Yoga Anusandhan Sansthan, Bangalore, Kaivallyadham Lonavala (Maharastra) and Brahmavarchas Śodha Ṣansthana, Shantikunj. They made the scientific aspects of Yoga very popular. On the basis of scientific researches they have shown how Yoga can be useful in our day to day life.

SCHOOLS OF YOGA

Yoga has two origins, one from Vedas and the other from Tantras. The Tantras developed a philosophy and a set of practices which in the Tantric tradition are known as *Yogaçhara,* conduct for people who practice Tantra through Yoga. The Vedic tradition describes Yoga in the form of the Upaniśads. Each Upaniśad represents a line of learning, a tradition, a *parampara*. Yoga became the process encompassing the body and the mind leading to the experience of spirit. This is how the Vedic and Tantric traditions viewed Yoga in ancient India.

In the present scenario there are only two established schools of Yoga: the Southern School and the Northern school. Yoga as taught and practiced by ṛśis, munis and tapasvis in the Gangetic belt, the Narmada belt and the Himalayan Belt was known as the Northern school. The Southern school was the Yoga practiced and envisioned by the southern group of sadhus and saints, renunciates and recluses, mystics and siddhas.

Today the main propagator of the Southern School of Yoga is T. Kṛśnamacharya, the teacher of Deśikachar and Iyengar. The Southern school believed by attaining total physical perfection. Hatha Yogis also believes in this principle.

The Northern school is more meditative, having as its basis the 'Yoga Sutras' of Patanjali. In the 'Yoga Sutras', the emphasis is on mind management, thought management, and Hatha Yoga finds very little mention. Patanjali's Yoga is recognized as the Northern School of Yoga.

In the Northern School of Yoga there are different *Paramparas* (Tradition or culture). There is even a tradition of Hath Yogis. There is a tradition of Kriya Yogis, a tradition of Kundalini Yogis; there are not only Raja Yogis but also Jnana Yogis and Bhakti Yogis. All these Yogis had one thing in common: Yoga, a practice and discipline through which it becomes possible to strengthen one's nature, to realize the human spirit, and to awaken the inherent potential to become a balanced, perfect human being. Human being can attain perfection in one thing, in all the expressions of life. To attain this end many branches developed in the Northern School of Yoga.

Fifty years ago, the philosophical side of Yoga was known to a few people, but nobody knew the practical side. It was believed that Yoga was meant for sadhus and sannyasins who had renounced everything and had left the pursuits of the world for a life of contemplation, meditation, reflection, introversion and isolation; that it was a way to salvation which an ordinary person in society could not adopt without renouncing some major attachments, desires, ambitions and efforts in life. Yoga was known as a philosophy only, as a form of discipline which could be utilized to strengthen one's spirit, mind, body and life. The theoretical knowledge was brought to the public by Swami Vivekananda, Śrī Aurobindo, Raman Maharśi, Baba Ram Das, Swami Sivananada, Śrīram Sharma Acharya and others in this past century.

There are over a hundred different schools of Yoga. Some of the most well known are as follows:

Bhakti Yoga: The practice of extreme devotion in one-pointed concentration upon one's concept of God.

Karma Yoga: All movement, all work of any kind is done with the mind centered on a personal concept of God.

Jnana Yoga: The path of wisdom; considered the most difficult path.

Hatha Yoga: The physical movements and postures, plus breathing techniques. This is what most people associate with Yoga practice.

Raja Yoga: Called the "royal path," because it incorporates exercise and breathing practice with meditation and study, producing a well-rounded individual.

Tantra Yoga: A way of showing the unseen consciousness in form through specific words, diagrams, and movements. One of the diagrams that is used to show the joining of the physical and spiritual bodies is two triangles superimposed upon one another. The downward-pointing triangle represents the physical body, or the female aspect having to do with work, action, and movement; the upward-pointing triangle represents the spiritual body of support, energy, and vastness.

Kaśmir Śaivism: This Yoga system states that everything in the universe has both male and female qualities. In Kaśmir Śaivism, these male and female principles form an equal partnership, so interdependent that they cannot be separated. The attraction between them produces the ultimate union of opposites, creating the immense complexity of the universe that we enjoy and celebrate. Unlike other philosophies, Kaśmir Śaivism is based in emotion rather than intellect. In fact, Śaivism says that intellectual understanding by itself will never lead us to the realization of the summit of Yoga. The system's great exponents teach that the egotistical intellect blocks our ability to fully experience our individual power.

JÑĀN YOGA

The word **Jñān (Gyan)** literary means knowledge and wisdom, and thus it is known as Yoga of Knowledge or wisdom. What is that knowledge? It is understanding or experience of the self. To know the self through knowledge or wisdom is Jñān Yoga.

This path of Yoga deals directly with the highest of all human desires—the desire to know the Truth—and it gives an explanation of what Truth means and shows the practical way of realizing it. Truth is not the subject to change, death, decay and destruction. It never changes at any time; it was never born, and will never die. It is self-existent and does not depend on anything. Gyana Yoga is the science that provides a systematized and organized method of study in order to fulfill this desire to know the Truth.

The truth or reality is only ***Atman*** the knowledge of self, which is ultimate. To know that and to know the importance of that *Atman* Lord Kṛśna says in The Gita:

// Na Jāyate Mriyate Vā Kadāçhinnāyam Bhūtwā Bhavitā Vā Na Bhūyah /
/ Ajo Nityah Śāśwatoayam Purāno Na Hanyate Hanyamāne Śarīre //

—Śrīmadbhagvad Gīta2/20

Meaning: This is never born, nor does it die. This is unborn, eternal, changeless, ever-Itself. It is not killed when the body dies.

When the aspirant becomes aware of this ultimate truth he starts realizing the self and starts following the path of JñānYoga and ultimately gets liberated from all worldly bondage of Karma. In this sense lord Kṛśna again says in Gīta that:

// Karmajam Buddhiyuktā Hi Phalam Tyaktwā Manīśinah /
/ Janmabandhavinirmuktāh Padam Gaçhçhhantyanāmayam //

—Śrīmadbhagvad Gīta2/51

Meaning: The aspirant of JñānYoga after knowing the ultimate truth possessed of this evenness of mind and abandoning the fruits of their actions, freed for ever from the fetters of birth and go to that state which is beyond all evil that is ***Mokśa***.

Hence all the Sadhana in which Intellect or knowledge is used as object is JñānYoga; as The Holy Gita describes JñānYoga with the name of Samkhya Yoga, but basically the sadhana of Vedanta is known as JñānYoga; since in Vedanta the knowledge is the main path of Yoga through which the aspirant becomes one with Brahma.

According to the principle of JñānYoga the Atman is ***Ananda śwarūpa*** (as blissful), ***Jñānśwarūpa*** (knowledge form), ***Sat*** (truth), ***Nitya*** (forever), ***Suddha*** (pure) and ***Buddha*** (intellect). In the real sense the Atman is Brahma it self. Only Brahman is the reality, there is no existence except it.

Brahman is self-focused, endless, uninterrupted, unborn, conscious and blissful. As the fire is one and reflects in different form in several places, the same is the case with Brahman, it is one but appears in the form of soul of every creatures and it is beyond all of them.

According to JñânYoga the knowledge of unity of ***Jiva*** (the individual being) and ***Brahman*** (the Supreme Being), bring the aspirant to the state of Mokœa, the liberation. In other words the knowledge of Brahman and liberation from all the worries is Mokœa it self. According tc this tradition it is possible only when the oneness of Jiva and Brahman has been proved. It has been said that the aspirant of higher level is able to know that reality only through listening the ***Srutivakya*** (the sayings of Brahman). He is able to remove the difference between Jiva and Brahman. According to Vedanta this reality is possible only through Knowledge.

JñānYogi

The practice of JñānYoga is divided into two paths: ***Antaranga*** practice and ***Bahairanga*** practice. *Bahiranga* (external) practice includes ***Viveka, Vairagya, Śatśampati*** and ***Mumukśutva***; whereas the *Antaranga* (internal) practice includes ***Sravana, Manana*** and ***Nidhidhyasana***.

Viveka (Discrimination): The practitioner has to develop and cultivate the ability to recognize what is impermanent, temporary and fleeting in life as the Sadhaka experiences the fact—what is of everlasting value and pointing to the eternal. The practitioner becomes able to discriminate the superficial and the essential; as well as the illusory reality on the surface and the absolute reality in the inner, deep dimension of existence. In this way, the person tries to scrutinize, analyze and evaluate constantly the experiences, inclinations, decisions and actions.

Vairagya (dispassion): In the practice of Vairagya the practitioner has to guard his mind against becoming possessed, infatuated and even slightly disturbed by passions springing from the sensual desires. Later on he has to stop all the disturbances like attachment to things that bring sensual satisfaction. The opposite of Vairagya is ***Raga*** (passion) which means originally colouring, which indicates that passions are, in fact obstructions of the mind which do not allow clear vision. To achieve the clarity of mind (which is essential for final knowledge and wisdom) attachments and passions must be renounced.

Satsampati (Six-attainments): This discipline includes a six fold instruction of self-education for success on the path of Yoga which are:

- *Sama:* The cultivation of tranquility of the mind.
- *Dama:* Self control in action
- *Uparati:* Means eradicating the eagerness to possess.
- *Titikśa:* To have patience
- *Sraddha:* Confidence (in the meaning of faith).
- *Samadhana:* Intentness of the mind.

Mumuksutva (longing for liberation): This fourth Sadhana of Vedanta is very important. It should be understood as the immense desire to get the higher level of consciousness i.e. Samadhi. The Sadhaka or aspirant should develop a positive desire for liberation. Its development is supported by the previous endeavors as the advanced ability to discriminate the unsatisfactory superficial reality and the safety-promising, spiritual dimension of higher experience. The practice leads towards ultimate reality i.e. ***Brahman***.

In JñānYoga in the practice of Antaranga the first one is ***Sravana*** which means hearing. The practitioner has to go first through an extensive and intensive study, for which one should go to his Guru (the spiritual teacher or master) and should listen to the lesson on (about) Brahman. In ancient time it was done in Ashrams (the traditional school of Vedanta or Yoga), now a days it includes thorough studies of the traditional doctrines of the Vedantic texts or Upaniśads. This gives to the mind of the aspirant the right direction and outlook and material for the second stages which is ***Manana***.

Manana starts with intellectual analysis of the material gained by studying the texts. The analysis of the material gained by knowledge of the world of sensual and emotional experience and on the level of speculative thinking, final knowledge cannot be found. Absolute truth can lie only beyond them. When the practitioner firmly arrives at this conclusion, he is able to enter the path of meditation which brings him to the subsequent and final stage of training which is ***Nidhisyasana***.

This expression can be translated as constant meditation. This stage of training makes it clear to the Sadhaka that the process of opening a new channel to reality over and above the senses and the intellect is not a matter of mental exercises during meditational session only, but that it is also equally necessary to introduce a kind of meditational atitude towards one's life so that eventually the mind is in a state of meditation even when dealing with the business of everyday life. As this capacity is developed and deepened, the Yogi's intuition and spiritual vision grow until he reaches the final vision of truth, which brings the aspirant to the final achievement of liberation or ***Mokśa***.

BHAKTI YOGA

Bhakti Yoga is the easiest and natural way for God-realization. It is deeply concerned with our life. This path of devotion is for everyone. Anybody can practice it. Even the vilest man can do this and gradually improvement will take place soon. The ***Narada Bhakti Sutra*** defines Bhakti in the second verse as follows:

// Sā Tvasmin Parama-premarupā //

Meaning: Bhakti is the supreme love for Him (God). The object of real devotion is only God and nothing else. This love should be pure and powerful; there should not be any kind of selfishness associated with it. And one should not expect or think of anything like wealth, prosperity or any worldly object from God—not even happiness.

The Bhagwad Gita discusses the ***Bhakti Yoga*** as an easier path of Yoga. The Gita says that when a devotee's love for God reaches its climax, his love for God is known as the Yoga of devotion. The devotee wants nothing in return; and when he loves God in such a way his love takes the form of Yoga which is called the Yoga of devotion or Bhakti Yoga.

In the twenty second verse of the eighth chapter, Lord Kṛśna reflects the Yoga of Devotion when He says:

// Puruśah Sa Parah Pārth Bhaktyā Lavhyastwananyathā/
/ Yasyāntah Sthāni bhūtāni Yen Sarvamidam Tatam //

Meaning: O'Arjuna, that eternal unmanifest supreme Puruśa in whom all beings reside and by whom all this is pervaded, is attainable only through exclusive Devotion.

The twenty sixth verse of the ninth chapter highlights how a devotee with his pure love wins the heart of the Lord.

// Patram Puśpam Phalam Toyam Yo me Bhaktyā Prayaçhhati /
/ Tadāham Bhaktyupaçhatmaśnāmi Prayatātmanah //

Meaning: Whosoever offers to me with love a leaf, a flower, a fruit or even water, I appear in person before that disinterested devotee of sinless mind and delightfully partake of that article offered by him with love.

When we go through the seventeenth verse of the twelfth chapter we find what lord Kṛśna Himself says about devotion:

> *// Yo Na Haśyati Na Deśti Na Śoçhati Na Kānkśati /*
> */ Śubhāśubha Parityagi Bhaktimānyah Sa Me Priyah //*

Meaning: He who neither rejoices nor hates, nor grieves, nor desires and who renounces both good and evil actions and is full of devotion, is dear to me.

The final aim of Bhakti is the communion of individual consciousness with supreme or Universal consciousness. But before we come to this stage, there are different stages of Bhakti which act at the deeper level of mind to transform the mental structure, the mental conditioning. **Goswami Tulsi Das** explains the nine steps of Bhakti in **Śrī Rām Çharita Mānasa** (Rāmāyana) in a very specific form as:

> *// Navadhā Bhagati Kahaun Tohi Pāhin /*
> *Sāvadhān Sunu Dharu Mana Māhin //*
> *//Pratham Bhagati Santanh Kar Sangā /*
> *Duśari Rati Mam Katha Prasangā//*

Satsanga (associate with truth or the company of truthful person) is considered to be the first form of Bhakti. Being near a saint and having their Satsanga, instruction and guidance can be one form of Bhakti. Another form of the same Bhakti can be taken as analyzing the Truth and spiritual life; but whatever it is the main emphasis is on one's being in the company of Truth. Now, if we also define this psychologically, the Truth here represents a quality which is gained after attaining discernment. If there is no discernment, there can be no discovery of Truth. So, in order to experience Truth one needs to have the power, the force of discrimination.

One can attain this form of Bhakti through Sadhana, whether that Sadhana is being in the company of a person who is enlightened, absorbing his of her vibrations and allowing the inner mind to experience it, or whether that Sadhana is self-analysis, trying to develop the faculty of discernment through a meditative process or way of life. According to their level of life and consciousness, everyone has to give their own definition to Satsanga, or be in the company of Truth.

The second form of Bhakti is *Katha Prasanga*, which in colloquial language is listening to *Lilas* or story of divine beings. These Lilas about enlightened beings can help inspire us to accept a different lifestyle, mentality and mode of behaviour. However, it also has a psychological meaning. It is the nature of the mind to involve itself in constant gossip and criticism. The moment one stops the mind from gossiping and criticizing, it becomes calm, peaceful and fixed. It begins to experience a different kind of personal nature, which has no attraction towards the world of senses and objects. That is the experience of *Śūnyata*, the void, awareness of a different quality manifesting.

// Gur Pad Pankaj Seva Tīsari Bhagati Amān/
/Çhauthi Bhagati Mam Gun Gan Karai Kapat Taji Gān//

The third form of Bhakti is *Amān*, becoming egoless. In order to be egoless it is necessary to have Vairgya and live in world, but not be of the world. In fact, the entire philosophy of the Bhagwad Gita is based on this very principle—one should do his own work, should perform own Dharma, carry out all obligations, but should not think that he is the indispensable one. One should not have any attachment. One may be attached to something, whether to a person, or to the results of an action. Wherever there is even the slightest inkling of attachment, there is a connection with ego. Possessiveness, desire, ambition are all involved in attachment. To be egoless is to give a different vision of life where we are able to experience the state of non-being.

The fourth form of Bhakti is *Japa*. Japa, literarly means continuous repetition of a Mantra or God's name. It is constant remembrance that, whoever lives in this body, the individual self and the cosmic self which pervades the entire universe, is one. In *Japa*, the essence has to be realized. A raindrop and water in the river or ocean are two different things, but they are composed of the same essence or matter. *Japa* is the process of identifying with the Divine or cosmic nature. It is a method by which a person who has attained viveka and vairagya can disassociate the individual self from the manifest dimension and link with the cosmic dimension:

// Mantra Jāp Mam Drirh Biśwasā /
/Panċham Bhajan So Bed Prakaśa //

The fifth form of Bhakti is *Bhajana*—incorporating the transcendental, humanitarian and unconditioned qualities into everyday life. The qualities which we express in our lives are conditioned qualities which gave some restrictions and motivations in them. The real language of living is expressing these qualities which are cosmic, divine and human, which are not conditioned, but which are free from every kind of mental or manifest impression. When one is free from the attractions and repulsions of life, love is experienced. So, removing the conditions which we create in the expression of a quality is the fifth form of Bhakti.

// Çhhath Dam Sīl Birati Bahu Karma /

Nirat Nirantar Sajjan Dharma //
// Sātavam Sam Mohi Maya Jag Dekha /
Moten Sant Adhika Kari Lekha //

The sixth form of Bhakti is the 'total involvement' in *Sajjan Dharma*, i.e. manifesting in one's life the qualities which are divine and human while following one's dharma. Generally, when we live a quality life, we tend to isolate ourselves from the dharma belonging to the realm of the body, the realm of the mind and emotions, and also from the dharma governing the spiritual dimension. It sounds easy, but we find it very difficult to combine the principles of spirituality and awareness with the normal, external environment and life style. Instead of feeling the rejection and repulsion inside, instead of identifying with a personal desire, live life from moment to moment by accepting situations as they come up, and follow dharma accordingly.

The seventh form of Bhakti is *seeing the spark of life and divinity in each and every one.* There should be no distinction between one and another. There should be no concept of high and low, but there should be identification. Seeing the divinity within self as well as other beings, whether animate or inanimate, is the highest form of compassion where the individual self is totally eradicated *(Kaput)*

// Āthavam Jalāthābh Santośa /
Sapnehun Nahin Dekhai Pardośa //
// Navam Saral Sab San Çhhalhīna /
Mam Bharosa Hiyan Haraśa Na Dīna //

The eighth form of Bhakti is *contentment*, not seeing fault in other beings. One who does not struggle, or fight, who does not see any kind of fault in other people, but who lives and flows with life, is content. If there is acceptance of the natural law then there will be no criticism. Everyone is following His law, to develop the acceptance, is one of the important form of Bhakti.

The ninth form of Bhakti is *Atma nivedana–total surrender, total fusion or total merger.* Atma means self and nivedan means to offer. It happens when even the last vestige of individual identity is dissolved in cosmic awareness. At that level the body becomes God. The state of Atma Nivedan is not very easy to attain. If faith becomes powerful and takes that real experience where the existence ceased to this world this will be the state of Atma Nivedan.

// Nav Mahun Ekau Jinh Ken Hoī /
Nari Puruśa Saçharaçhar Koi //

The ninth forms of Bhakti is not only for the fulfillment of only the requirement but these can lead to discrimination and ultimately the final state i.e. Samadhi the goal of Yoga.

Bhakti is of two types—*Para* and *Apara*. As we go on, in the prepartory stage, we unavoidably stand in need of many concrete helps to enable us to get on, and indeed the mythlogical and symbological parts of all religions.

When Bhakti has reached its peak, it is called the Para, no more is there any fear of hdeous manifestations of fanaticism. In the words of Swami Vivekananda: The one great advantage of Bhakti is that it is the easiest and the most natural way to reach the great divine.

KARMA YOGA

The Karma comes from Sanskrit root *'kri'* which means to do. Karma literary means action, which every one performs in this world, whether consciously or unconsciously. The human beings have a natural tendency to perform some thing. The Gita says:

// Na Hi Kasçhit Kśanmapi Jātu Tisthatya Karma Krit
Kāryate Hyavaśah Karma Sarvah Prakritijairgunaih //

—Śrīmadbhagvad Gīta2/5

Meaning: No person can stop his activity at any time even for a moment, because the entire humanity has been forced by the Nature to perform action.

Karma is the expression of the rule of perfect justice within us. It is the law of the cosmos reflected in the microcosm. There is nothing arbitrary or punitive about it. It is universal law and inevetable fact. All the phenomena of Nature are governed by one important law, the universal law of causation, which is also known by the name 'the Law of Karma'. The law of causation is a universal law that keeps up the inner harmony and the logical order of the universe. Man's deeds are subject to this law.

No success can be attained without understanding the law of Karma. The three aspects of the law of Karma should clearly be grasped. The first is the ***Sançhita Karma***, the sum total and stored actions, good or bad in the innumerable past lives that we have left behind. The whole of it is recorded and preserved. The second is ***Prarabdha Karma***, the inevitable Karma. It is that portion of our Karma which is assigned to us to be worked out in a single life in relation to men and things we met and experienced in previous lives. The third form is that of ***Kriyamana Karma***. It is that Karma which is in the course of making. It is that which preserves our free-will with certain limitations and ensures our future success.

One cannot do anything with past Karmas unless he is fully enlightened. With knowledge of the Divine, the enlightened ones create the fire of knowledge that burns all the bondages created by past Karmas. That is possible but unless one has that ability, he has to reap the consequences of his past Karmas.

Since birth to death human beings perfom Karma because of the bondage of the law of Karma. These Karmas are the causative factor behind the bondage of a person. Now the question arise— If Karma binds us and without doing Karma one cannot stop himself, then how can one be liberated? or there is no chance for liberation? The answer is—As the Karmas is the causative factor of Bondage, it can liberate the aspirant because it is the causative factor of liberation also. The second question arises as to what type of Karma bounds us and what kind of Karma can liberate? Lord Kṛśna replys Arjuna in The Gita as:

// Tasmaçhçhhāstram Pramānam Te Kāryākāryavyavasthitau /
/ Gyātwā Śāstravidhānoktam Karma Kartumihārhasi //
—Śrīmadbhagvad Gīta16/24

Meaning: Which Karma should be performed and which one should not, to distinguish it there is no reference in any text, you should act after knowing the view of authorised text.

One should perform Karma according to the need of the situation; the main thing is that one should be aware of his ***Kartavya*** (duty). One should perform his duty without any expectation. In this context the Gita says:

// Yagyarthātkarmanojanyatra Lokoyam Karmabandhanah /
/ Tadartham Karma Kaunteya Muktasangah Samāçharah //
—Śrīmadbhagvad Gīta 3/9

Meaning: The world is bound by actions other than those performed for the sake of Yagya, therefore O son of Kunti, you perform action for Yagya only. Here the Yagya means the action done for the sake of others or of selfless motive. The karma performed for others without any expectation, does not bind the aspirant. This selfless action is called Karma Yoga.

Karma Yogi

In the first stage of the Sadhana of Karma Yoga the aspirant performs his action with the feeling of Duty. Through the attachment to Karma or the result of Karma the person gets bounded with the Karma. Hence any obstacle in the path of Karma hurts the performer as the performer is attached to the fruits of Karma. When the aspirant gives up this attachment to the result he then becomes a Karma Yogi.

> *// Yuktah Karmaphalam Tyaktwā Śantimāpnoti Maisthikim /*
> */ Ayuktah Kāmakārena Phale Śaktwe Nibadhyate //*
>
> —Śrīmadbhagvad Gīta5/12

Meaning: The aspirant of Karma Yoga performs the karma for the realization without expectation whereas the Sakām Puruśa (general performer) binds them with the desire of result. Hence Karma Yogi does not attach himself to the success or failure. Without expectation, the mind becomes desireless and then he becomes free from attachments with the world. It may lead to liberation.

The question arises now—without expectation can the performer become inspirationless? But the answer is no. Hence the real inspiration will be with the desireless performer. To perform duty without any obstruction, the aspirant needs some codes of conduct, which seems to be very difficult but with the help of a ***Guru*** it becomes easier for the Karma Yogi. In the practice of Karma Yoga, the aspirant needs a Guru, in whom he has full faith. It is also important here that the aspirant should have strength of resolution and full dedication to his Guru. Faith and resolution makes the path of Yoga easier.

Mantra-Çhudāmanyopniśad says that the disciple should have the following charcteristic features with him: pure mind, good character, faith in Guru, dedication to the path, and added to these he should be an optimist. With all these virtues the aspirant of Karma Yoga becomes closer to the God. He is able to perform the karma and offer it to God, and this is the theme of Karma Yoga. Lord Kṛśna says the same thing in the Gita as:

// Yatkarośi Yadśnāsi Yajjuhośi Dadāsi Yat /
/ Yatta Pasyasi Kaunteya Tatkuruśwa Madarpanam //

Meaning: O' son of Kunti (O' Arjuna) whatever action you perform like *Yagna, Tapa or Dana,* offer it to me and then you will be free from the bondage of their results.

Karma Yoga in real sense makes one get the freedom which is the goal of human beings. Every unselfish action takes us towards the goal. Most of the human beings in this world follow the path of Karma Yoga consciously or unconsciously. Those who know that the path of Karma is like worship of the Lord, perform their actions skillfully, selflessly, and lovingly.

Karma Yoga is a very effective and valid path of Yoga in order to experience the total self. One who is in control of the self and who is devoid of desire is a true renunciate. A true renunciate easily attains enlightenment in this path.

RAJA YOGA

The word Raja Yoga is found in many of the Upaniśads. It may be regarded as the master of all the yogic practices. All the yogic practices lead to Samadhi, but the speciality of this path is that it starts from Samadhi. Hence the Samadhi comes in every path, thus it has been considered to be the complimentary practice of Yoga or the greatest path of Yoga.

The importance of Raja Yoga has been accepted very widely. The Great Hatha Yogi Swatmarām also says in Hatha Pradipika as:

// Kevalam Rājyogāya Hthavidyopnidiśyate //

—Hatha Pradipika ½

Meaning: the lession of Hatha Yoga is only for the attainment of Raja Yoga.

There are various definitions of Raja Yoga, Yoga Swarodaya defines it as:

// Yathākāśe Bhraman Vāyurākāś Vrajate Swayam /
/ Tathākāśe Manolīna RajaYoga Kriyāmatam //

Meaning: Just as the air passing through sky never appears, likewise to establish the mind in ***Sunya*** (No object) is Raja Yoga.

Yogaśikhopaniśad defines Raja Yoga as:

// Rajso Retso YogādrājYoga Iti Smritah //

Meaning: The *Raj* form of Kundalini when merges with *Ret* form of Śiva or the union of ***Atma tattwa*** (individual self) with ***Brahma Tattwa*** (the supreme self) is Raja Yoga.

A careful observation of the the above mentioned definitions shows that the establishment of the self in Brahman is Raja Yoga. In this state the practitioner becomes one with Brahman; the dualism destroys and this is the aim of any path of Yoga. For the practitioner the world disappears; and the practitioner gets rid of all miseries of the world and he is established in the self.

The practitioner of Raja Yoga has been divided into three kinds: the first type is ***Uttam*** or the advance practitioner, second type of Raja Yogi is called ***Madhyam*** or the medium and the third one is called ***Adham*** or the beginners. This categorisation also differentiates the practice of the individual.

The **Uttam** type of practitioner needs a special type of package for the Attainment that is *Abhyas* and *Vairagya*. Maharśi Patanjali has also given the same instruction to them in his Yoga Sutra.

// Abhyās Vairāgyābhyām Tannirodhah //

—Patanjali Yoga Sutra 1/12

Meaning: There are two methods for stopping the flow of the *Çhitta vrittis*. First is ***Abhyāsa*** or continuous practice and the second one is ***Vairāgya*** or detachment from all the *Raga* and *Dwesa* (liking and disliking)

The next thing is *Iśwarpranidhan*, It has been said that the advance practitioner can attain the Samadhi through ***Iśwarpranidhan*** only. In this context Maharśi Patanjali says in his Yoga Sutra:

// Samadhi Siddhiriśwar Prānidhānāt //

—Patanjali Yoga Sutra 2/45

Meaning: One can attain success in Samadhi by complete resignation/ surrender to God. Here the word Samadhi is not exactly that; it is a state of Trance. In this state the aspirant loses the body awareness and becomes able to start with deeper awareness.

Hence the aspirant is here of high quality, he need not practice the other steps. He can start from Samadhi onward. Such Yogis already have completed their Sadhana in past lives.

The Second type of Practitioner (***Madhyam***) has been instructed to practice ***Kriya Yoga.*** This type of aspirant needs a few more hard practices as he also has past life practice but in lower form. Thus for him Patanjali describes ***Kriya Yoga*** as:

/ Tapah Swadhyayayeśwarpranidhānāni KriyaYogah /

—Patanjali Yoga Sutra 2/1

Meaning: *Tapa* (penance) *Swadhyaya* (Self study) and *Iśwarpranidhan* (faith in God) constitutes Kriya Yoga. Tapa literary means to burn, here Tapah means the Sadhana of optimum level where all the past karma burns and the aspirant illuminates the imperfection.

The aspirant of medium class needs to develop the mastery over Summer-winter, Pain-pleasure, and contempt-respect etc. The mind then is able to remain stable in all the stages. Aspirant starts studying the self the inner self *(Swadhyaya)* and it leads towards surrender to God (*Iśwarpranidhan)*. These three things lead the aspirant to attain the Samadhi.

The beginners or Adham Sadhaka those who did not start the Sadhana has been suggested to adopt Astanga Yoga (eight fold path). Maharśi Patanjali says in his Yoga Sutra:

// Yamaniyamāsanāprānayāmapratyāhāradhāranā
dhyānsamādhayostāvangāni //

—Patanjali Yoga Sutra 2/29

Meaning: Yama, Niyama, Asana, Pranayama, Pratyahara, Dharana, Dhyan and Samadhi are the steps of Astanga Yoga. They need to practice all the steps as their body and mind both need a preparation and suppleness for Samadhi.

In the practice of Raja Yoga the aspirant requires the practice to attain the Samadhi according to his level. Elsewhere Raja Yoga is also known as Dhyan Yoga, because ultimately the aspirant has to reach that state where Samadhi is easier to attain. In this context Dharana, Dhyan and Samadhi come in series and is called Samayama together.

// Trayamkaetra Samyamah //

—Patanjali Yoga Sutra 3/4

Meaning: When Dharana (Concentration), Dhyan (Meditation) and Samadhi becomes one this state is called Samyamah or Discipline. This discipline is, necessary, no doubt but at the same time regularity too, is essential for the aspirant.

Now the question arises if the every Sadhaka or aspirant has to reach Samadhi only then what is the difference among them? There are different levels of Samadhi, too which has been suggested to different levels of Sadhaka.

We have the description of the four kinds of Raja Yogi in ancient texts. They are as follows: the First is ***Prathama Kalpita***, the second one is ***Madhu Bhumika***, and the third one is ***Madhu Pratika*** and the fourth is ***Atikrānt bhananiya***. Among them ***Pratham Kalpita*** is said to be the newly arrived they need to practice the ***Savitarka Samādhi.*** The second type of Yogi which is said to be at a better level is the ***Madhu Bhumika***, they need to have the practice of ***Nirvitarka Samādhi.*** The third type of Raja Yogi which is known as ***Madhu Bhumika*** is said to be better and so both of them need to practice the ***Asmitānugat Samadhi.*** The best level of Sadhaka or ***Atikrānt Bhananiya*** Yogi has already attained the mastery over ***Ritambharā-Pragyā*** and over ***Asmitānugata Samādhi.*** Through the regular practice of that he experiences ***Asampragyāt Samādhi.***

When the Sadhaka or aspirant becomes able to govern the ***Çhittavritti*** (mental fluctuation) of mind and attain ***Ritambhara- Pragyā,*** he becomes one with his ***Karana Prakriti*** or the subtle self and Atman gets liberated and thus attains the ***Kaivalya*** (the Ultimate reality).

Thus it can be said that Raja Yoga is the only practice of Yoga which is open for all, and easier to adopt also. Only through the practice of Raja Yoga, Atman comes know the real self.

II

Introduction to Hath Yoga

Normally people understand Hath Yoga as doing yogic postures and mastering them forcefully, whether it takes a lot of energy or makes the practitioner exerted. But it is definitely not so. The word 'Hath' has been used in Yogic texts and ancient literature in a different meaning. It has been defined as:

> *// Hakāra Kīrtitah Sūryasya Thakāra Çhandra Uçhyate /*
> */ Sūryā Çhandra Masauryogād Hathayogo Nimadyate //*

> *Meaning*: The word 'Hatha' is made up of two Bīja Mantra: '*Ha*' and '*Tha*'; where '*Ha*' represents Sun or *Pingala Nadi* and '*Tha'* represents Moon or *Ida Nadi*. Basically the union of these two *Nadies* is called Hatha Yoga. The another meaning of these two Bīja can be understood as follows; '*Tha*' represents Prana, the vital energy and '*Ha*' represents mental energy. So Hatha Yoga means the union of the pranic and mental forces.

When *Ida* and *Pingala* unites together the Prana starts flowing into Suśumnā and the dormant power ***Kundalini*** which is lying in the ***Mūlādhāra Çhakra***, rises and enters *Suśumna* and passing through all the six *Çhakras* reaches the highest peak ***Brahmarandhra*** or ***Śahaśrāra***, and attain the oneness. This is the union of ***Śakti*** and ***Śiva*** or *Atman* and *Parmatman*; this process destroys the ignorance of the aspirant and illuminates his heart and soul. Thus the process of this union is called Yoga.

The aim of Hatha Yoga is to have mastery over body and mind. The main objective is to create an absolute balance of the interacting and processes of the physical body, mind and energy. When this balance is established the impulses generated give a call of awakening to the central force which is responsible for the evolution of human consciousness.

Hatha Yoga Pradipika is one of the most authentic text books on Hatha Yoga, written in 1200 AD by Swami Swatmarama, a great Yoga Guru who formulated the principles of Hatha Yoga and systematically explained various techniques, its effects on body, mind and states of consciousness. This is a comprehensive text on Asanas, Pranayama, Cleansing techniques, Mudras (Mental attitude or gestures), Bandhas (Energy locks), Nada (Sound) Meditation and many more guidelines for following the path of Yoga.

Swami Swatmarama was the follower of Natha Tradition, (followers of Adi Nath or Lord Shiva), taught by great Gurus like Gorakshanath and then Matsyendranath. This is the tradition of sages who live in caves or Himalayas and renounce material life adopting sanyasa.

Whereas **Gheranda Samhita** another text of Hatha Yoga explains the process in seven steps in details as:

> *// Śodhanam Dridhtāçhaiva Sthairya Dhairyam Çha Lāghavam /*
> *Pratyakśam Çhā Nirliptam Ghatastha Sapta Sādhanam //*

Meaning: These are the following steps: ***Śodhanam*** (purification), ***Dridhtā*** (Suppleness of body), ***Sthairya*** (Stillness of body), ***Dhairyam*** (patience), ***Lāghavam*** (lightness of body), ***Pratyakśam*** (Facing the troubles) and ***Nirliptam*** (detachment) of ***Ghatastha Sapta Sādhan*** (seven steps of the perfection of body) which should be practiced by the aspirant of Hatha Yoga.

How to attain this perfection, for that Maharśi Gheranda explains the ***Saptanga Yoga*** (seven steps of Yoga) as:

> *Śatkarmnā Śodhanam Çha Āsanena Bhaved Dridham / Mudrayā Sthirtā Çhaiva Pratyāhārena Dhīratā //*
> *Prānāyām Lāghavam Çha Dhyānāt Pratyakśamātmane /*
> *Samādhinām Çha Nirliptam Mukti Raiva Na Sanśayah //*

Meaning: The practice of śatkarma purifies the body. Asanas makes the body strong, Mudras bring stillness in the body; Through the practice of Pratyāhāra one acquires patience, Pranayama makes the body of Sadhaka or aspirant light and by the practice of Samadhi the mind get detached; there is no doubt about it. The above mentioned seven steps of Yoga should be understood in detail.

Hatha Yoga is also known as the science of purification as it includes six types of cleansing process. In order to purify the mind it is necessary for the body as a whole to undergo a process of absolute purification. This purification or Śatkarma are: ***Dhauti, Neti, Basti, Nauli, Trataka*** and ***Kapalbhati***. Here is the brief introduction of all six processes of Purification.

After the practice of Śatkarma the next practice is **Asana**. Hence Patanjali Yoga Sutra defines Asana as ***Sthiram Sukham Asanam*** (stillness and comfortable posture is called Asana) but in Hatha Yoga it is a specific position which opens the energy channels and psychic centers. When Prana or energy flows freely, the body also becomes supple. Stiffness of the body is due to blockages and accumulation of wastes.

It is said that it should be of eighty-four lakhs types but it doesn't seem practical. We find the description of eighty-four types of Asanas. Maharśi Gheranda describes thirty-two types of Asana. Among them Padmasana, Siddhasana, Swastikasaṇa, Vajrasana, Pasçhimottanasana are common. Siddhasana is said to be the best for Sadhana, as ***Siddhasana*** stops the downfall of energy levels, and is useful for spiritual awakening.

Thereafter the practice comes in Hatha Yoga is Mudra. ***Mudra*** is the specific gesture of the body. Hatha Yoga Pradipika discusses ten Mudras whereas Gherand Samahita mentions twenty-five types of Mudra. Jalandhar Bandha, Mūla Bandha, Uddiyana Bandha, Maha Bandha, Maha Mudra, Kheçhari and Viparītakarnī Mudra are common among them.

Hatha Yogic Texts give a lot of importance to the practice of Pranayama. It is very clearly said that for the perfection in Sadhana of Hatha Yoga Pranayama should be practiced after Asanas. Texts describe ***Astakumbhaka*** (eight fold practice of Pranayama) i.e. Surya Bhedi, Ujjai, Bhastrika, Bhramari, Śītali, Śitkari, Murçhha and Plavini. Through the practice of Pranayama body becomes light weighted, all the *Nadies* become purified and the mind becomes stable.

Now comes the practice of Dharana, Dhyan and Samadhi which are the assets of any Sadhana. Practice of Dhyan or meditation is of four types as mentioned in Hatha Yoga; Padastha, Pindastha, Rūpastha and Rūpātīta. There is the description of two types of specific Meditation, they are Saguna and Nirguna Dhyan. Practice of Dhyan leads to Self-realization and through the regular practice of that Dhyan the mind becomes detached and it is the state of Samadhi. The aspirant can attain Mokśa or Kaivalya. Swami Swatmaram explains the aim of Hatha Yoga in Hatha Pradipika as:

// Kevalam Rājyogāya Hthavidyopnidiśyate //

—Hatha Pradipika 1/2

Meaning: the lesson of Hatha Yoga is only for the attainment of Raja Yoga or the ultimate reality.

The same thing is repeated at the end of the text as follows:

// Sarve Hathyopāyā RājaYogasya Siddhaye //

—Hatha Pradipika 4/103

Meaning: All the practices and clues given in Hatha Yoga is only for the attainment of Raja Yoga.

SHATKARMA

Hatha Yoga, as described in the early Yoga Upanishads, was made up of the Shatkarmas and is a very precise and systematic science. *Shat* means 'Six' and *karma* means 'Action'; Shatkarmas consist of six groups of purification practices. The aim of Hatha yoga and, therefore, of the Shatkarmas is to create harmony between the two major Pranic flows, Ida and Pingala, thereby attaining physical and mental purification and balance.

All Shatkarma techniques purify not only the physical body but affect its subtle components, so that to ensure safe and successful progression along the spiritual path. Therefore, even if you were attracted by asana, pranayama, or meditation in the beginning, very soon you will understand that without the inner purification you cannot go farther. It is no wonder that the yogis who have attained perfection consider the Shatkarma with great esteem. The six kriyas according to Gheranda Samhita and Hatha Yoga Pradipika are: Dhauti, Vasti, Neti, Thataka, Nauli and Kapalbhati.

Dhautir-vastis-tatha netir, tratakam, Naulikam tatha/
Kapal-bhatis-c-aitani, Sat-karmani samacharet //

—Gheranda-Samhita, 1/12

Dhautir bastis tathā netis trātakaṃ naulikaṃ tathā/
kapāla-bhātiś chaitāni ṣat-karmāni prachakṣate //

—Hatha Yoga Pradipika, 2/22

Maharśi Gherand systematically explains the Śatkarma in detail. The First Śatkarma is **Dhauti**. This means to clean and in Gheranda Samhita it is said to be of four types: ***Antaradhauti, Dantadhauti, Hridadhauti*** and ***Mūlaśodhan***.

Antaradhauti literally means internal organs cleansing. It is of four types again, *Vātsār, Vārisār, Vahnisār* and *Bahiśkrita*. ***Danta Dhauti*** means dental cleansing, which is also of four types: *Danta Mūla, Jihwa Mūla, Karnarandhra* and *Kapālrandhra*. ***Hrida Dhauti*** means cleansing of heart region and it is of three types: *Danda Dhauti, Vaman Dhauti* and *Vastra Dhauti*. The fourth Dhauti is ***Mūla Sodhana***, which is the cleansing of anal region.

The second process is Neti. It should be understood as the nasal passage cleansing. Basically it is of two types: ***Jala Neti*** and ***Sutra Neti*** according to Gheranda Samhita. Somewhere there is the description of *Dugdha Neti* and *Ghrita Neti* also.

The next cleansing process is Basti. It is the cleansing of lower abdomen or rectum only. It is of two types according to Maharśi Gheranda: ***Jala Basti*** and ***Pawan Basti***.

Later comes the practice **Nauli**. It is the movement of abdominal muscles and it is of three types: ***Dakśina Nauli, Vāma Nauli*** and ***Madhya Nauli***.

Trataka is the cleansing of eyes. According to Gheranda Samhita it is of two types: ***Vahya*** and ***Ābhyantar***.

The last process is **Kapalbhati** and it is also of three types: ***Vātakrama, Śītakrama*** and ***Vyutakrama.***

Practice of Śatkarma mentioned above is not necessary for all aspirants; it is for those who need the inner cleansing. This means the aspirant doesn't have balanced three Dośas (Vāta, Pitta and Kapha), or Sapta Dhātus are not in balance. The practice of Śatkarma brings a balance among them.

The Shatkarmas are also used to balance the three humours in the body: Kapha (Mucus); Pitta (Bile); and Vata (Wind). According to both Ayurveda and Hatha Yoga, an imbalance of the humours will result in illness. These practices are also used before Pranayama and other higher yoga practices in order to purify the body of toxins and to ensure safe and successful progression along the spiritual path. These powerful techniques should never be learned from books or taught by inexperienced people. According to the tradition only those instructed by a guru may teach others. It is thus essential to be personally instructed as to how and when to perform them according to individual needs.

As Astānga yoga emphasises on Yama and Niyama, Hatha yoga emphasises on cleaning process, that is Kriyas, Only a healthy and clean body can have a healthy and clean Mind. The yogic kriyas or cleansing practices are six in number and hence called shat-karma (six-actions).

When the different systems of the body have been purified of toxins, the harmony in the energy channels (nadis) is created and the overall result is that energy can flow freely through the body, thereby attaining emotional purification and balance and the brain works much more effectively. When all components of the body are well balanced the mind becomes more stable.

ASANA

Swatma Rama the author of Hatha yoga Pradipika defines Asana as: ***"Kuryattadasanam sthairyamarogyam cangalaghavarn."*** This implies that Asanas should result in stability and absence of disease, as well as contributing to lightness of the body and feeling of well being. Following practices are basically for the physical fitness though they have their spiritual effects and other Hatha yogic benefits.

According to Gheranda Samhita, Shatkarma is the first step of Hatha Yoga, but According to Hatha Yoga Pradipika, Asana is the first step of Hatha Yoga:

> *Hathasya prathamāìgatvād āsanaṃ pürvam ucyate |*
> *Kuryāt tad āsanaṃ sthairyam ārogyaṃ cāìga-lāghavam ||*
> —Hatha Yoga Pradipika, 1/19

Meaning: Before everything, Asana is spoken of the first step of Hatha Yoga. Having done Asana one gets steadiness of body and mind and he will be free from every disease and a feeling of lightness in the body can be experienced by the practitioner.

Āsanāni samastāni yāvanto jīva-jantavaḥ |
Caturaśīti lakśāni śivena kathitāni ca ||

—Gheranda Samhita, 2/1

Gheranda Samhita describes that according to the kinds of animals and creatures, there should be eighty-four types of Asanas, and among them 32 are important.

Teśām madhye martya-loke dvātrimśad āsanam śubham ||

—Gheranda Samhita, 2/2

Hatha Yoga Pradipika describes fifteen asanas which are mainly: *Svastikasana Gomukhasana, Vīrāsana, Kürmāsanạ, Kukkutāsana, Uttāna-kürmasana, Dhanur-āsana, Matsyendrāsana, Paścimatāna, Māyürasana, Shavāsana, Siddhāsana, Padmāsanạ, Siṃhāsana and Bhadrāsana.* These Asanas can be divided basically into two types: first type of asanas for making the body supple and the second type of asanas to support the meditation.

Asanas are not just physical exercises: they have biochemical, psycho-physiological and psycho-spiritual effects. The cells of the body have their own intelligence and memory. Through practice of different asanas blood circulation is improved, the hormone system is balanced, the nervous system is stimulated, and toxins are eliminated, so that the cells, sinews and nerves are kept at their peak level. Physical, mental, and spiritual health and harmony are attained.

Siddham padmam tathā bhadram muktam vajram ca svastikam |
Simham ca gomukhạm vīram dhanurāsanam eva ca ||
Mṛtam guptam tathā mātsyam matsyendrāsanam eva ca |
Gorakśam paścimottānam utkatam saìkatam tathā ||
Mayüram kukkutam kürmam tathā cottāna-kürmakam |
Uttāna-mandukam vṛkśam mandukam garudam vṛśam ||
Salabham makram cośtram bhujaìgam yogam āsanam |
Dvātrimśad āsanāny eva martye siddhi-pradāni ca ||

—Gheranda Samhita, 2/3-6

Gheranda Samhita mentions thirty-two types of Asanas which are as follows: *Siddhasaṇa, Padmamasana, Bhadrasana, Muktaasana, Vajrasana, Svastikasana, Simhasana, Gomukhasana, Vīrasana, Dhanurāsana, Mṛtasana or Shavasana, guptasana, matsyasana, matsyendrāsan, Gorakśasana, Paścimottāna, Uutkatasana, Sankatasana, Mayūrasana, Kukkutasana, Kūrmasana, Uttāna-kūrmasana, Uttāna-mandukasana, Vṛkśasana, Mandukasana, Garudasana, Vṛśasana, Salabhasana, Makrasana, Bhujaìgasana* and *Yogāsana.*

Importance of Asana can be understood as they are for the health and balance of the body, have a deeper purpose: to diffuse the consciousness uniformly throughout the body, so that duality between senses, nerves, cells, mind, intelligence and consciousness are eradicated, and the whole being is in harmony. When the nervous, circulatory, respiratory, digestive, endocrine and genito-excretory systems are cleansed through asanas, prana moves unobstructed to the remotest cells and feeds them with a copious supply of energy.

According to Hatha Yogic Texts Asanas are the bases for advancement in Yoga. The practical aspect of Asana has been described in last chapter of the same book, which will support the aspirant as a guide.

PRĀNĀYĀMA

The word Pranayama is made up of two words: Prana and Ayama. Prana is the vital energy and ayama means expansion of the pranic energy. Swami Swatmarama in Hatha Yoga Pradipika talks about Pranayama as the way to awaken the kundalini, regular practice of Pranayama can lead to spiritual awakening and self realization. He describes various types of Pranayama, which has different effects on the body, mind and spirit.

Pranayama has been mentioned as Kumbhaka in Hatha Yogic Texts. It is the fourth step of the eight-fold Yoga described by Patanjali. The credit for making the practice of pranayama popular as a discipline in its own right and as a means for maintaining the health of the body and mind goes to the followers of Hathayoga. They gave it a place of great importance among the practices of Hathayoga.

Athātaḥ sampravakśyāmi prānāyāmasya sad-vidhim |
Yasya sādhana-mātrena deva-tulyo bhaven naraḥ ||

—Gheranda Samhita, 5/1

Gheranda says that the practice of Pranayama leads the aspirant to the level of God. Authors of Hatha Yoga describe various techniques of pranayama, emphasizing the utility of each of them. There are instructions to practice them separately and comfortably.

Sūrya-bhedanam ujjāyī sītkārī śītalī tathā |
Bhastrikā bhrāmarī mūrcchā plāvinīty aṣta-kumbhakāḥ ||

—Hatha Yoga Pradipika, 2/44

Hatha Yoga Pradipika explains eight types of pranayamas and their effects, but cautions that just as a trainer of lions, tigers or elephants study their habits and moods and treat them with kindness and compassion, then put them through their paces slowly and steadily, the practitioner of pranayama should study the capacity of his lungs and make the mind passive in order to tame the incoming and outgoing breath. If the animal trainer is careless, the animals will maim him. In the same way, a wrong practice of pranayama will sap the energy of the practitioner and may even cripple him.

Sahitaḥ sürya-bhedaś ca ujjāyī śītalī tathā |
Bhastrikā bhrāmarī mürcchā kevalī cāśta kumbhakāh
—Gheranda Samhita, 5/46

In Hatha Yoga Pradipika and Gheranda Samhita pranayamas has been mentioned as Astha Kumbhaka i.e. eight types of pranayama; But both the text having their own astha kumhaka, although some of them are common but few are different. Apart from that there are some specific practices mentioned in other texts, so all together have been mentioned below:

1. *Nadi Shodhan Pranayama means Nadi Purifying Pranayama*—This particular pranayam should be taken as pre pranayama practice. As according to its nature it purifies the all subtle energy channels called Nadis. This practice balancing the Ida and Pingala, the mental force and vital force is one of the main objectives of Pranayama. Left nostril (Ida) and right nostril (Pingala) if balanced can awaken Sushumna (the psychic nadi or channel carrying kundalini) nadi. Swami Swatmarama recommends Nadi Shodhan Pranayama, (alternate nostril breathing with Kumbhaka and Bandhas) for purifying Ida and Pingala Nadis.
2. *Sahit means "Combined"*: There are two types of sahita pranayama: first one is Sagarbha which means "with seed" and second one is Nigarbha, which menas "without seed". There are lots of benefits of this pranayama discussed in Yogic Texts. Practice of this pranayama leads to Levitation; it cures diseases; it awakenes Shakti; brings calmness, bliss of mind; exaltation of mental powers (e.g. clairvoyance).
3. *Surya Bhedan means "Sun-piercing"* to practice the pranayama breath in through right nostrill. Hold the breath inside and adopt Jalandhar Bandha so long as "the perspiration does not burst out from the tip of the nails and the roots of the hair" (According to Gheranda). Exhale through left nostril. This practice destroys decay and death; awakens Kundalini shakti; increases body fire (Gheranda); cleanses the brain and sinuses (Svatmarama). This Pranayama

stimulates the sympathetic nervous system and left part of the brain. It eliminates wind or gas related trouble (Vata Dosha as per Ayurveda) and balances Mucus (Kapha as per Ayurveda) and Bile / acidity (Pitta Dosha as per Ayurveda).

4. *Ujjayi means "Victorious"* : This is also called psychic breath. This type of Pranayama is done with inhaling via nostrils, then performing Bandhas and exhaling through left. During inhalation and exhalation a typical sound (Ujjayi Sound) should be created by compressing epiglottis in the throat. Ujjayi sound can be combined with So-Ham or Guru Mantra for better awareness of Mantra. Ujjayi Pranayama has therapy applications, especially useful in insomnia, tensions, and heart diseases. This should not be practiced in Low blood pressure, as the practice of this Pranayama puts pressure on carotid sinus which further reduces blood pressure. It may even lead to death.
5. *Bhasrika (bellow's breath)*: This literally means one has to operate lungs like the bellow, fast inhalation and fast exhalation, followed by inhaling through right nostril and performing kumbhaka with bandhas and exhaling through left nostril, this is is Bhasrika Pranayama. This is vitalizing type of Pranayama. This rhythmic inhalation and exhalation stimulates the circulation of cerebral fluid, creating compression and decompression in the brain. Rhythmic diaphragm movements stimulate heart and lung muscles improving blood circulation. Accelerated blood circulation and rate of gas exchange in each cell produces heat and washes out gases. This practice purifies energy channels (nadis); the practitioner never suffers from any disease; it stimulates gastric fire; and later on the kundalini rises quickly, it pierces the three "knots" (granthi) in sushumna (i.e. Brahma, Vishnu, Rudra), which allows the prana to ascend sushumna (Svatmarama).
6. *Bhramari menas Humming Bee Breath*: In this Pranayama one has to make sound like humming bee while exhalation and inhalation as well. According to Gheranda Samhit this should be done at the mid night. To practice it close the ears with the hands. Listen to the sounds in the right ear. Listen for sounds of crickets, lute, thunder, drum, beetle, bells, gongs, trumpets, etc. The last sound heard is the "unstruck" (anahata) sound rising from the heart. In this sound is Light, and in that Light the "mind should be immersed." This Pranayama increases psychic sensitivity and awareness of subtle sound vibrations, and this proves to be useful for Nada Mediatation. This is useful in removing stress and mental problems like anxiety, depression, anger etc. This practice gives success in Samadhi and indescribable happiness.
7. *Sitkari means "Making the [sound] sit"*: This is done by opening

lips, keeping the upper and lower teeth touching each other, then inhaling through mouth with hissing sound, then performing kumbhaka with bandhas and then exhaling with nostrils. The air passing via tongue, cools the blood, lowering the temperature of the blood. This type of Pranayama removes excess heat in the body. Also the diseases like acidity, hypertension etc. This Pranayama harmonizes the secretions of reproductive organs and all the endocrine system. Also it improves digestion, lowers High Blood pressure, purifies the blood. Accoding to Swatmarama the practitioner becomes "next to the God of Love (Kama) in beauty" (Svatmarama); it removes heat, hunger, indolence, sleep, and thirst.

8. *Shitali means "Cooling"*: To follow this practice, we have to imitate the breathing of a serpent. Curl the tongue and protrude it through pursed lips (kaki-mudra) then inhale through mouth with a hissing sound. Tongue is rolled and inhalation is done via mouth followed by Kumbhaka with Bandhas and then exhalation with nostrils. The effects of the Shitali are same as Sitkari Pranayama. This is the "Giver of bliss"; it makes free from indigestion, phlegm, and bilious disorders; purifies blood; cools system; quenches thirst, appeases hunger.
9. *Moorcha means Swooning Breath or Fainting*: This type of Pranayama induces a state of "conscious unconsciousness" (in the words of Swami Satyananda of Bihar School of Yoga). One should inhale through both the nostrils, the kumbhaka with Bandhas, but while exhaling the Jalandhar Bandha (Chin Lock) is kept intact and then exhalation is done with the Jalandhar bandha (Chin lock). Excess pressure is exerted on carotid sinus during exhalation with Jalandhar bandha, which further reduces blood pressure and one can experience a state of unconsciousness with practice. This Pranayama involves high risks and so should not be.practiced without the direct guidance of a yoga teacher.
10. *Plavini is Floating Breath*: After inhalation the air is filled into stomach and kept inside for some time. When the belly is filled with air and the inside of the body is filled to its utmost with air, the body floats even on the deepest water, like the leaf of a lotus. Swami Swatmarama mentions in the text of Hatha Yoga Pradipika that one can float easily on water with this Pranayama. This Pranayama helps in removing most of the ailments of stomach or digestive system.

Kumbhaka (Retention of air) along with Bandhas (energy locks) is very important in Pranayama, it has long lasting effects on nervous system, brain and other parts of the body. But the guidance of a guru is essential for practicing Pranayama. The practice of Kumbhaka increases the oxygen in the blood, which stresses the nervous system, and continuous practice results in nervous system becoming tolerant. Some of the Yogis have displayed unique capacity to survive without oxygen, with regular practice of Pranayama.

MUDRĀ-BANDHA

Bandha means lock and mudra means seal. The human system has many apertures or outlets. By locking and sealing these, the divine energy known as kundalini is awakened and finds its union with purusa in the *sahasrara* chakra.

Mudras and bandhas act as safety valves in the human system. Asanas act in a similar way. All three help to suspend the fluctuations of the mind, intellect and ego, so that attention is drawn in towards the Self. The union of the divine force with the divine Self is the essence of Part Three.

In order to follow the technique of Pranayama, it is necessary to know something about mudras, and bandhas. The Sanskrit word mudra means a seal or a lock. It denotes positions which close the body apertures, and where the fingers are held together with special hand gestures.

Bandha means bondage, joining together, fettering or catching hold. It also refers to a posture in which certain organs or parts of the body are gripped, contracted and controlled. When electricity is generated, it is necessary to have transformers, conductors, fuses, switches and insulated wires to carry the power to its destination; otherwise the current would be lethal.

When prana is made to flow in the yogi's body by the practice of pranayama, it is equally necessary for him to employ bandhas to prevent the dissipation of energy and to carry it to the right places without damage. Without the bandha, the pranayama practice, and the flow of prana can injure the nervous system.

Mahā-mudrā nabho-mudrā uddīyānam jālandharā |
Mūlabandho mahā-bandho mahā-vedhaś ca khecarī ||
Viparītkarī yonir vajrolī śakti-cālanī |
Tādāgī māndukī mudrā śāmbhavī panca-dhāranā ||
Aśvinī pāśinī kākī mātaìgī ca bhujaìginī |
Pancavimśati-mudrāś ca siddhidā iha yoginām ||

—Gheranda Samhita, 3/1-3

Meaning: Mahā-mudrā, Nabho-mudrā, Uddīyān, Jālandharā, Mūlabandha, Mahā-bandha, Mahā-vedha, Khecarī, Viparītkarnī, Yonī, Vajrolī, Shakti-cālanī, Tādāgī, Māndukī, Shāmbhavī, Aśvinī, Pāśinī, Kākī, Mātaìgī and Bhujaìginī, are the twenty five Mudras, which gives perfections to the Yogis.

Out of the several mudras mentioned in Hatha-yogic texts, jalandhara, uddiyana and mula bandha are essential for pranayama. They help to distribute energy and prevent its waste through hyper-ventilation of the body. They are practiced to arouse the sleeping kundalini and direct its energy up through the susumna channel during pranayama. Their use is essential for experiencing the state of samadhi.

Jalandhar Bandha

The first bandha the sadhaka should master is jalandhara bandha, jala meaning a net, a web or a mesh. The solar plexus is situated at the center. According to Yoga, it is the seat of the digestive fire (jagharagni), which burns food, and creates heat. The lunar plexus is in the center of the brain and creates coolness. By performing jalandhara bandha, due to the lock of the nadis around the neck, the cool energy of the lunar plexus is not allowed to flow down or to be dissipated by the hot energy of the solar plexus.

In this way the elixir of life is stored. And life itself is prolonged. The bandha also presses the ida and pingala channels and allows the prana to pass through susumna. The jalandhara bandha clears the nasal passages and regulates the flow of blood and prana (energy) to the heart, head and the endocrine glands in the neck (thyroid and para-thyroid).

If pranayama is performed without jalandhara bandha, pressure is immediately felt in the heart, brain, eye-balls and in the inner ear. This may lead to dizziness. It relaxes the brain and also humbles the intellect (manas, buddhi and ahamkara).

Those with stiff necks should keep the head as far down as possible without undue discomfort, or roll a piece of cloth and place it on the top of the collar-bones. Hold it by lifting the chest rather than by pressing down with the chin. This releases tension in the throat and breathing becomes comfortable.

Uddiyana Bandha

Uddiyana Bandha, which means flying up, is an abdominal grip. In it, the prana or energy is made to flow up from the lower abdomen up into the thorax, pulling the abdominal organs back and up towards the spinal column.

It is said that through uddiyana bandha the great bird prana is forced to fly up through the susumna nadi, the main channel for the flow of nervous energy, which is situated inside the spinal column (merudanda). It is the best of the bandhas, and he who constantly practices it, as taught by his guru, lives young for a long time.

It is said to be the lion that kills the elephant named death. It should be performed only during the interval between a complete exhalation and a fresh inhalation. It exercises the diaphragm and abdominal organs. The lift of the diaphragm gently massages the muscles of the heart, thereby toning them. It tones the abdominal organs, increases the gastric fire and eliminates toxins in the digestive tract. As such it is also called sakti chalana pranayama.

Moola Bandha

When the muscles of the perineum are contracted, the whole pelvic floor is pulled up. The perineal/vaginal region or 'yoni' is pressed and the rectum is contracted. The word Tudam indicates 'rectum'; but it also means anus, bowels, or lower intestine. However, it should be clearly understood that in mula bandha, there should be absolutely no anal contraction.

Contraction of the anus is known as ashwini mudra. Ashwini mudra indicates the movement a horse makes with its rectum during evacuation of the bowels. In the Gherand Samhita it is said to contract and relax the anal aperture again and again.

When mula bandha is initially practiced, there is a tendency to control the two areas, i.e. the perineum and the anus. Mula bandha takes place in the center of the body, neither in the front nor back. Then mula bandha chakra is directly contracted. In the beginning the student will find difficulty in asserting conscious control over the perineal area, as the brain is not tuned to such fine muscular manipulation in this area.

The practice of mula bandha reactivates the areas in the brain controlling this region of the body, bringing the neuronal circuits responsible for its control into the sphere of consciousness. This growth process takes time, and in the meantime, while practicing mula bandha, it is important not to become frustrated if you cannot control the perineal body, or the cervix, without contracting the anus or genital organs also. In the initial stage this is to be expected. Controlled systematic contraction of the perineal body/cervix produces heat in the body, and this awakens the potential of kundalini. Control will definitely come with time, practice and perseverance.

III

Introduction to Pātanjal Yoga

CONCEPT OF CHITTA AND ITS MODIFICATIONS: CHITTA VRITTI

Chitta is derived from the Sanskrit rootword chit, which means to see, to be conscious of, or to be aware. *Chitta* is the Subconscious mind. It is the mind-stuff. It is the store-house of memory. Samskaras or impressions of actions are imbedded here. It is one of the four parts of antahkarana. Hence Chitta means individual consciousness, which includes the conscious state of mind, the subconscious state of mind and also the unconscious stare of mind. The totality of these three states of individual mind is symbolized by the expression Chitta.

Chitta has been differently accepted in Vedanta, but here Chitta represents the whole of the individual consciousness, which is comprised of three stages: the sense or objective consciousness, the subjective or astral consciousness, and the unconsciousness or mental state of dormant potentiality. The verb chitta means to perceive, to know or understand. 'Chitta' as a noun means thought, vision etc.

The process of modification which the objects undergo between the region of the mind and the Buddhi or *Mahat* (intellect) is called *vritti*. The psychic medium termed vritti always operates between the knower and the known. The *Purusha* (the spirit) is subjected to enjoyment and sufferings in the material world due to these *chitta vrittis* (functions of the mind). As a result the individual ego becomes restless and it is mainly due to five kinds of afflictions such as avidya (absence of true knowledge), *asmita* (wrong identification of the Self with mind and body), raga (attachment), dvesha (aversion) and abhinivesa (fear of death and instinctive affinity to life).

Yogaś cittavṛttinirodhaḥ ||

—Patanjal Yoga Sutra (1/2)

Yoga is defined as the *chitta vritti nirodha* which means cessation of all the fluctuations of the mind. This restraint over the mind is attained through various steps of the yoga discipline.

Mandukyopnishad Conveys the four stages of consciousness; i.e. *Jagriti* (awakened) *Susupti* (sleep) *Swapna* (dream) and *Turiya* (Bliss) the state of dream is the subtle world of *Parmatman* which is in between awaken and sleep state of consciousness.

> *Jagariasthaano Bahishprajnah saptaanga Ekonavinshatimukhah sthoolabhugvaishvaamarah Prathamah Paadah.*
>
> —Mandukyopanishad (3)

The first aspect is the waking state, the awareness of external things, the terrain of aishvanara. He had seven limbs and nineteen mouths, and his enjoyment lies in the visible objects of the world.

> *Svapnasthaanoantah Prajnah Saptaanga Ekonavinshatimukhah Praviviktabhuktaijaso Dviteeyah Paadah.*
>
> —Mandukyopanishad (4)

The dreaming state is the second aspect, over which Tejas rules. Seven limbs and nineteen mouths belong to him, and the objects he enjoys are invisible.

> *Yatra supto Na kanchana Kaamam Kaamayate Na Kanchana Svapnam Pashyati Tatsushuptam; Sushuptasthaana Rkeebhootah Prajnaanaghana Evaanandamayo Hyaanandabhuk Chatomukhah Praajnastriteeyah Paadah.*
>
> —Mandukyopanishad (5)

The third aspect is deep dreamless sleep, which lies beyond desire. Prajna is the Lord of this territory; he lives in deep sleep in which all things have vanished, and he enjoys bliss. Prajna lies at the gateway to the dreaming and waking states.

> *Naantahprajnam Na Bahisnprajnam Nobhayatah Prajnam Na Prajnaanaghanam Na Prajnam Naaprajnam; Adrishtam Avyavahaaryam Agraahyam Alakshanam Achintyam Avyapadeshyam Ekaatmapratyayasaaram Prapanchopashamam Shaamtam Shivamadvaitam Chaturtham Manyante Sa Aatmaa Sa Vijneyah.*
>
> —Mandukyopanishad (7)

Turiya, is the fourth aspect. He remains unaware of the external, intermediate, and internal worlds. He lies beyond bliss consciousness and unconsiousness; it is indescribable. Not thought. *Turiya* enjoys pure awareness and experiences peace, bliss, and non-duality. He is none other than *Atman*; Realize Him.

In conclusion it can be stated that *Chitta* is the memory bank, which stores impressions and experiences, and while it can be very useful, Chitta can also cause difficulties if its functioning is not coordinated with the others.

A good way to cultivate the awakening of *Chitta* is to simply be aware of the streams of thoughts, emotions, images, and impressions that arise in front of Manas (on which *Manas* may or may not act). Notice how the stream of thoughts comes from somewhere, and then recedes back into that same place. This place is *Chitta*.

Now the question arises as to what is *vritţi*? In yoga the fluctuations of consciousness, the waves of mental activities can be understood as vritti.

There are five Vrittis according to Patanjali, which are as follows:

Pramäna-viparyaya-vikalpa-nidrä-smṛ tayaḥ ||

—Patanjal Yoga Sutra (1/6)

Pramāna means right knowledge, *Viparyay* means wrong knowledge, *Vikalpa* means options, *Nidrā* means sleep and the *Smriti* means the memory, these are the five vrittis, which are the real fluctuations of *Chitta*.

If *Chitta* is not coordinated with the other functions of mind, the thousands, millions, or countless impressions in this bed of the lake of mind start to stir and arise. It is as if these many latent impressions, coming to life are all competing for the attention of *Manas* to carry out their wants in the external world. In the absence of a clear *Buddhi*, the competing voices of *Chitta* often drive *Manas* to take actions in the world that are really not so useful.

INTRODUCTION TO PĀTANJAL YOGA

Sage Patanjali didn't discover Yoga Sutrā for mind game. These Sutrās have been authored to understand the practical process of uplifting the levels of consciousness to search the possibilities of mind and ultimately go beyond them. Yoga Sutrās are basically practice oriented. They don't only discuss the Samadhi intellectually but do give the practical knowledge and tools.

Several Sutrā explains those facts, which are beyond the worldly experiences. Yoga sutrā cannot be understood at mental level but the aspirants of Yoga who practice it. They need to get help to understand the vast depth of mind and Prāna. They understand it with experience. These Sutrās help the practitioner to reflect the path and to proceed carefully. Thus to understand them intellectually is neither possible nor relevant. As on the long root, the path of Yoga, the Yoga Sutrā plays the same role.

Statue of Maharshi Patanjali

Yoga Sutrā contains 195 verses; Sutrā literally means thread. Here, in Yoga Sutrā, this thread has been used to arrange the knowledge systematically like a garland, which is a complete philosophy in itself.

The text authored by Patanjali commonly known as *Yoga Darshan* means Philosophy of Yoga. *Darshan* came from Sanskrit root 'Dris' which literally means to see. Here, in Yoga Sutrā the word *Darshan* has been used only due to its ability to throw light on the path of Yoga. It can be stated that Yoga Sutrā develops the internal spiritual vision of the invisible wisdom. Yoga sutra can be taken as the best, appropriate and quite scientific text among all the Yogic texts authored till date. It has been divided into four chapters; Samādhi Pāda, Sādhnā Pāda, Vibhuti Pāda, and Kaivalya Pāda.

Samādhi Pāda contains 51 Sutrā which focus over following points: Definition of Yoga, Aim of Yoga, Vrittis, how to over come the Vrittis i.e. Abhyāsa and Vairagya, the objects of Samādhi, Ishwar Pranidhān, Chitta-Vikshepa, how to remove Chitt Vikshepa, Chitta Prasādan and its method as well as Savija and Nirvija Samādhi.

The second chapter Sādhanā Pāda contains 55 Sutras and they reflect the following subjects: Kriya Yoga—its practice and result; Pancha kleshas and the process to destruct them; Drishya (Prakriti) and Drastra (Purusha), their qualities, union and the process of overcoming them as well as to achieve the VivekaGyan; and the importance of yoga practice. This chapter also covers the Bahiranga Yoga, the first five steps of Astānga Yoga i.e. Yama, Niyama, Āsana, Prānāyāma and Pratyāhāra. These five steps of Astānga Yoga and their benefits for the aspirants are clearly mentioned in Sādhanā Pāda of yoga Sutrā.

Third chapter Vibhuti pāda contains 55 Sutras and this chapter focuses on the rest three steps of Astanga Yoga—commonly called Antaranga Yoga i.e. Dhārana Dhyāna and Samādhi; where as Vibhuti Pāda also mentions the Nirbija Samādhi and the bahiranga Sādhanā to attain that state i.e. Samyama. After that, the Pāda reflects in the results of *Chitta*; it also mentions all the objects related to Prakriti and its results. This chapter also mentions different Samyam and later on it discusses the Viveka Gyan i.e. Kaivalya.

Kaivalya Pada the last chapter containing 34 Sutrās; mentions the five ways to achieve Siddhis and its results, as well as the results of meditation i.e., overcoming the Sanskara and the secrets of Yogi's Karma. This chapter also discusses the Karma done by normal person, their types and the results. Later on this chapter reflects the subject of Viveka Gyan and ultimately what is Dharma Medha Samādhi and the state of Kaivalya.

The speciality of this text is that all the Sutra (verses) are arranged systematically and each one of them are to fulfill some specific aim at that point. Maharishi passes over from one sutra to another very wisely. Every word of these sutras is meaningful and significant in its own way.

All the technical words have been defined clearly in next sutras so that the aspirant should not face any difficulty in understanding. Sanskrit words have different and vast meanings, but in yoga sutra, the reader or practitioner gets the idea easily because of the clarification available in next sutra. In some places Maharishi has made this text short so that the aspirant can remember the sutras and there will be less chance of misconception. From the beginning to the end, Patanjali Yoga Sutra is filled with knowledge and wisdom.

ASTĀNGA YOGA

All spiritual activiteis are aimed at liberation of soul from the clutches of illusory name, form and identity and its reunion with its source—the universal consciousness. Astanga (eight-fold) Yoga is one of the most authentic paths of sadhana to achieve this end.

All the powers of mind like imagination, observation, decision-making, control, memory, and wisdom are activated by the pranic energy. Vivacity of senses is also possible by pranic energy only. All the intricate autonomous functions of the body and its organs are carried on without any conscious control of our own by this mysterious life force—the pranic energy.

Yamaniyamäsanapränäyämapratyähäradhäranädhyänasamädhayo'stäva aìgäni ||

—Patanjal Yoga Sutra (2/29)

To control and consciously utilize this life force for self-upliftment, purity and tranquility of mind and emotions are essential. To achieve this end, yam and niyam are two essential initial disciplines prescribed by the Astanga Yoga of Maharishi Patanjali.

Ahimsäsatyästeyabrahmacaryäparigrahä yamäḥ ||

—Patanjal Yoga Sutra (2/30)

Śaucasamtosatapaḥsvädhyäyeśvarapranidhänäni niyamäh

—Patanjal Yoga Sutra (2/32)

Non-violence, truth, non-stealing, celibacy and renunciation are called yamas and cleanliness, contentment, austerity, study of scriptures (spiritual texts), unwavering surrender to the will of God are called niyams. By following these disciplines the body becomes charged with energy, mind becomes cleansed and quiet and the sadhak is bestowed with will, zeal and faith to rapidly progress in his sadhana of self-awareness and self-realization.

Sthirasukham äsanaṃ ||

—Patanjal Yoga Sutra (2/46)

Along with yamas and niyams, the practice of Asanas (yogic postures) is third essential step so that one is able to sit in one posture for long hours without any uneasiness of body and mind.

Tasmin sati śväsapraśväsayorgativicchedaḥ pränäyämaḥ ||

- Patanjal Yoga Sutra (2/49)

The fourth step in this eight-step ladder of Astanga Yoga is Pranayam (control of breath). Normally the pranic energy in our ignorant state wildly dances to the tunes of passions and unbridled animal urges. Practice of Pranayam helps in calming them down and controlling these wayward and wild movements of the mind.

Svasvavisayäsamprayoge cittasya svarüpänukära ivendriyänäm pratyähäraḥ ||

- Patanjal Yoga Sutra (2/54)

Deśa-bandhaś cittasya dhäranä ||
Tatra pratyayaikatänatä dhyänam ||

- Patanjal Yoga Sutra (3/1-2)

Higher practices of pranayam are dangerous with an impure and disorganized mind and can even lead to acute mental disorders. hence advanced stages of pranayam should always be practiced with simultaneous practice of fifth, sixth and seventh steps of astang yoga sadhana i.e. pratyahar (withdrawal of senses), dharana (concentration) and dhyana (meditation). Without purification and control of the mind the prana sadhana remains a mere breathing exercise. It is beneficial to bodily health but it is not pranic yoga.

Sarvärthataikägratayoḥ ksayodayau cittasya samädhi-parinämaḥ ||
—Patanjal Yoga Sutra (3/11)

One has to learn the process of consciously focusing this energy for achieving the desired result. However the ultimate aim of the prana sadhana is the liberation of the enslaved individual being (prana) from the prison of the false ego identity and its union with the cosmic pranic being of eternal life, light and love- Samadhi—the eighth and the final step of Astanga Yoga sadhana. Persons endowed with abundance of this pranic energy are reckoned as truly great.

IV

Introduction to Human Body and Mind

The human body is a complex, highly organized structure made up of unique cells that work together to accomplish the specific functions necessary for sustaining life. Although viewed as a whole, the human body is actually made up of ten different systems. Each of these systems plays a vital part in the health and well being of the entire body.

SKELETAL SYSTEM

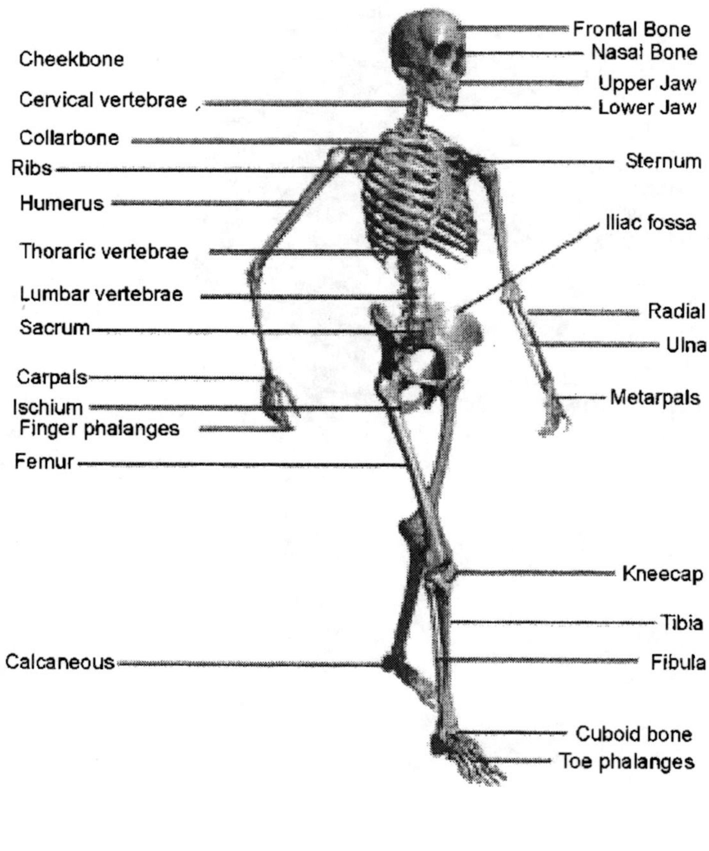

The skeletal system is the framework of the body. It is what gives the body its basic shape, while protecting the delicate internal tissues and organs. The joints of the skeletal system act as levers that are attached to various muscles. The elbows, knees, ankles are just a few examples of these levers. Another use of the skeletal system is that it acts as a storage area for calcium in case there is an inadequate amount available in the diet. A vital role of this system is also the production of red blood cells.

The skeleton is made up of 208 bones broken up into two different parts, the axial skeleton and the appendicular skeleton. The axial skeleton is comprised of the bones of the head and torso while the appendicular skeleton makes up the framework for the extremities.

MUSCULAR SYSTEM

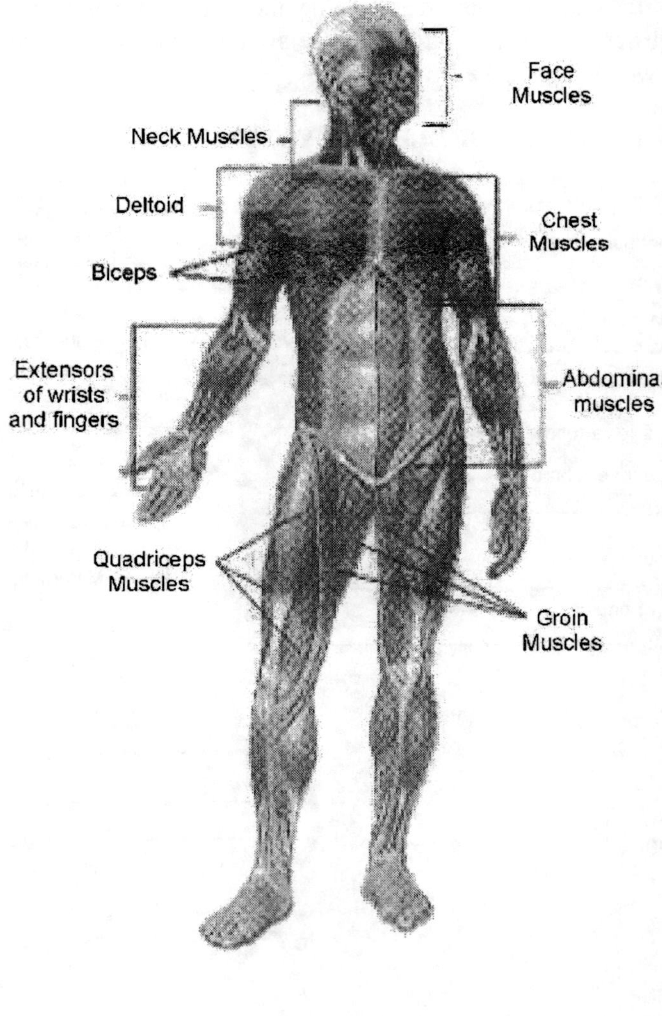

There are three types of muscle tissue that is included in this system, skeletal, cardiac and visceral. Skeletal muscles are voluntary muscles that work with the connective tissues to allow the body to move. Voluntary simply means the muscles respond to impulses from the brain that are a result of your desire to move.

Cardiac muscles are those that form the bulk of the heart's wall. They are known as the myocardium and are involuntary muscles. It is due to the cardiac muscles that the contractions know as heartbeats occur.

Visceral muscles are also involuntary. They are known as smooth muscles that is the walls of the viscera. Examples of visceral muscles are those that help move food along in the digestive tract, veins and arteries as well as the tubular structures of the urinary tract.

DIGESTIVE SYSTEM

The digestive system is comprised of all the organs that help break down food into a useable substance for the body. It includes the mouth, teeth, tongue, esophagus, stomach, duodenum, small and large intestines, colon, and rectum. It also includes accessory organs like the salivary glands, liver, gallbladder, pancreas and spleen.

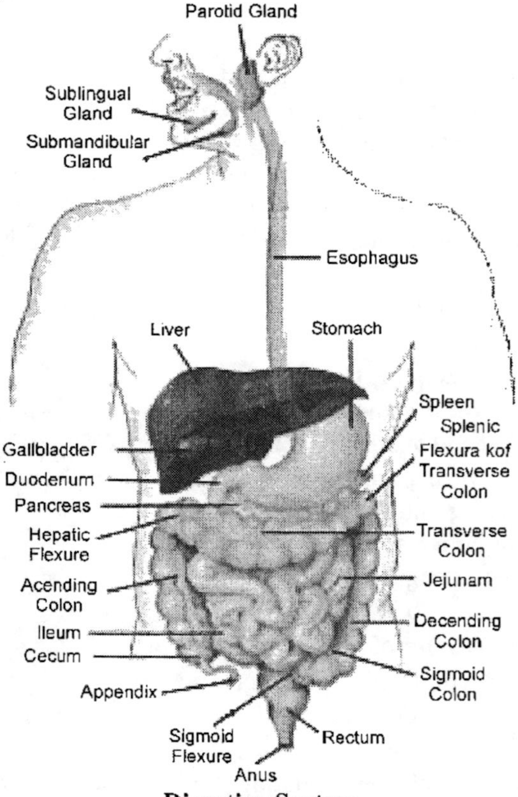

Digestive System

RESPIRATORY SYSTEM

The respiratory system is comprised of the lungs and the passages that lead to and from them. This system begins at the nostrils and includes the nasal cavities, sinuses, pharynx, larynx (voice box) and trachea (windpipe). Just before entering the lungs, the trachea branches into two bronchi that lead into the lungs. It is interesting to note that the right bronchus, which leads into the right lung, is noticeably larger than the left one. If a foreign object is accidentally inhaled, it is more likely to enter the right lung.

It is in the lungs that oxygen from the outside meets the blood by way of the thin tissues in the lungs. As the oxygen passes through the bronchi, it enters the bronchial tubes. When viewed from a cross section of the lungs, the bronchial tubes will resemble the limbs of a tree that grows progressively smaller with each branch. At the end of each of the tiniest branches of the bronchial tubes is a cluster of air sacs that resemble a bunch of grapes. Each of the alveoli is made up of a one-cell layer of flat cells and it is through these cells that the actual oxygen/blood mixture is done.

CIRCULATORY SYSTEM

The circulatory system is a closed system whose main function is to carry blood to all parts of the body. It is made up of the heart, arteries and systemic arterioles which carry oxygenated blood from the heart to the cells in the body as well as the systemic capillaries and veins which carry deoxygenated blood from the body back to the heart.

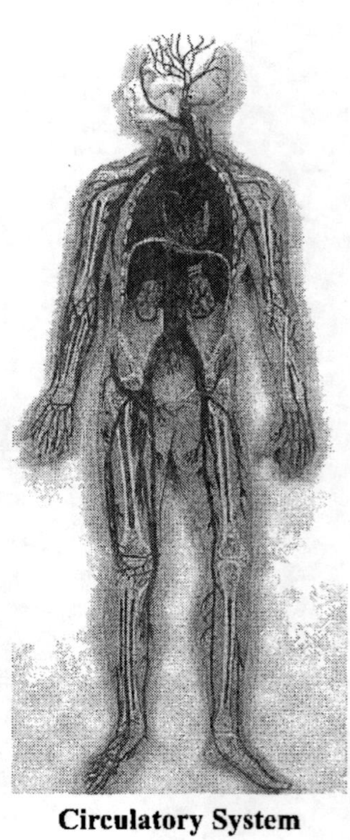

Circulatory System

SKIN

The integumentary system is the largest of all systems. It is comprised of the skin, hair, nails as well as the sweat and oil glands. It functions as a protective covering for the underlying tissues against drying and invasion by toxins or pathogenic organisms. The skin is also responsible for regulating body temperature.

The skin is made up of three distinct tissue layers. The epidermis is the outermost layer and is made entirely of epithelial cells. There are no blood vessels in the epidermis.

The dermis is the middle layer and contains many of the blood vessels, nerve endings and glands while the subcutaneous is the innermost layer. This layer is a combination of elastic, fibrous and adipose tissues.

NERVOUS SYSTEM

This is a very complex system by which all parts of the body are controlled. It is made up of the brain, spinal cord and nerves. It also includes special sense organs such as the eyes, ears and taste buds.

In itself, the nervous system is broken up into the central and peripheral nervous systems. The central nervous system is made up of the brain and spinal cord. The peripheral nervous system is made up of cranial and spinal nerves. There are twelve cranial nerves that carry messages to and from the brain. The spinal nerves are those that carry messages to and from the spinal cord.

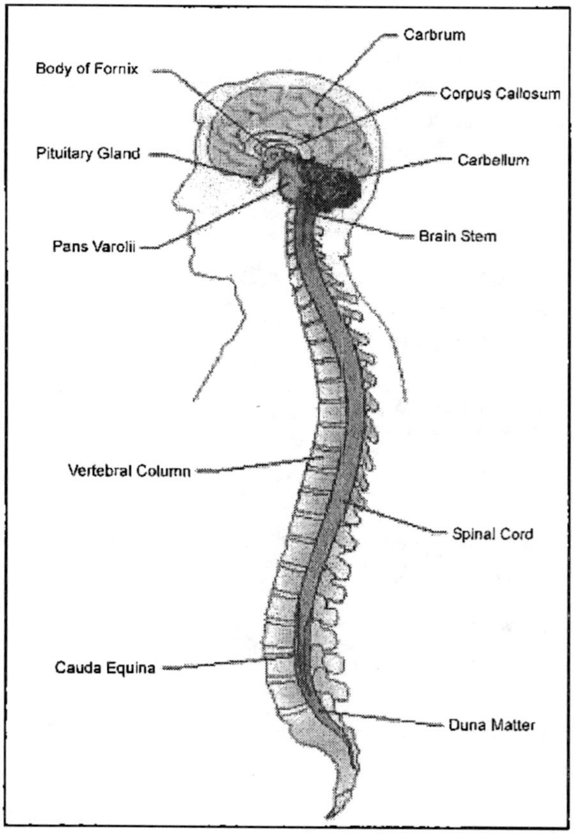

Nervous System

EXCRETORY (URINARY) SYSTEM

The excretory or urinary system is mainly comprised of the kidneys, the ureters, the bladder and the urethra. It the urinary system that filters out toxins and certain waste products that the blood has taken from the cells. Although certain toxins and waste products are also got rid of through the digestive and respiratory systems, they are considered separate systems.

REPRODUCTIVE SYSTEM

The reproductive system includes the external and internal organs as well as related inner structures that are required for the reproduction of another human being. These organs include the ovaries, testes, fallopian tubes, vas deferens, uterus, prostrate, urethra, penis, vagina, clitoris, vulva and labia.

ENDOCRINE SYSTEM

Although there are few parts in the endocrine system it is vital to the health of the individual. It is made up of organs called endocrine glands that produce hormones. These hormones in turn regulate growth, use of food within the cells and reproduction. The thyroid and pituitary glands are the two main endocrine glands.

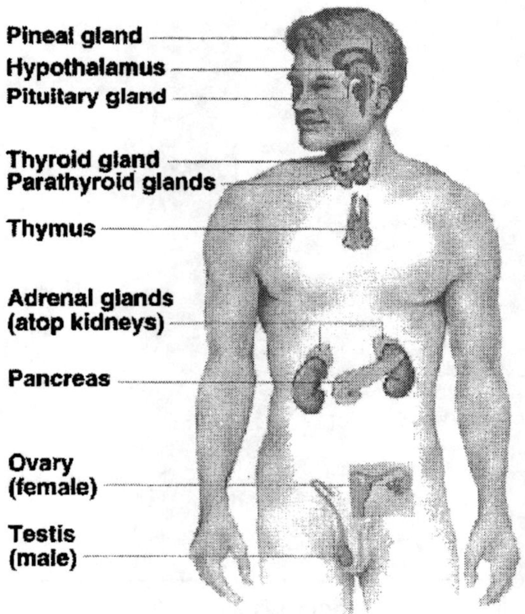

It is through these ten specialized systems all working together that allows us to maintain every aspect of life from standing to sleeping to breathing. If any one of these systems fail, the entire individual suffers.

EFFECT OF YOGIC PRACTICES ON HUMAN BODY

Yoga practices are life tuning process. It regulates our metabolic activities. Through subtle process of yoga our subtle body system is activated and therefore it regulates the physiology of our body, which reflects in new cells that are generated, and thus new powers are developed. Yoga ensures regular and complete blood circulation and this is the principle of biology that contraction and relaxation increases the body power by which diseases are eliminated from the body. Yoga affects us as a whole. As well as eliminating stress, charging the immune system and reducing age-related degeneration, it offers flexibility, strength and an increased understanding of how our body works. Below is a breakdown of the different ways yoga affects the body.

Skeletal System

Weight bearing exercises stimulate osteogenisis, or bone-tissue growth. So by holding your body in different ways, yoga postures promote bone strength in different areas. Standing poses, especially balances, creates and maintains joint stability in hips, knees, and ankles, while inverted postures such as Downward-Facing Dog builds stability in the shoulders. Twists and inversions keep the spine strong.

Yoga practice also builds up the muscles that support the skeleton. Chiropractors manipulates the joints of the spine to realign them, but if the muscle tissues that connect to the spine are not balanced and strengthened then the adjustment is only temporary. In the long run, treating the root cause of the misalignment is the safest method.

Muscular System

Yoga is one of the few physical practices that increases both muscular strength and flexibility. Research done in this area showed that after only 8 weeks of practicing yoga subjects' strength increased by 31 per cent, muscular endurance by 57 per cent and flexibility by 188 per cent. This has a direct impact on the quality of life: simple things like getting up from a chair, walking up stairs or opening a jar become effortless. Yoga offers protection from things like repetitive strain injury as it balances opposing muscles and stretches over tense ones. By maintaining a healthy, strong muscular system yoga makes movement easier, and protects against strain.

Digestive System

Most of the time we just let our digestion just get on with things. But we can help by stretching and developing muscles in the stomach and internal organs. Back bends pull the stomach away from oesophagus and the diaphragm—thus increasing tone and reducing the tendency to herniate. By stretching and manipulating our digestive system the intestines get massaged, peristaltic activity is improved and absorptive capacity is toned up. IBS and heartburn can managed by the gentle stretching and compressing of twists, massaging and increasing circulation to the area.

Respiratory System

Regular yoga practitioners have oxygen uptake levels equivalent to that of moderate athletes. Principally this is because yoga expands the elasticity of the inter-rib muscles, thus maximising lung capacity. This is especially the case in forward bends (which stretch the posterior part of the lungs) and pranayama which opens the alveoli (sacs that contain air in the lungs) and gas transfer is improved. Oxygen capacity usually diminishes with age as the ribs stiffen, but practicing yoga loosens these muscles, reversing the effects of age.

Circulatory System

Yoga strengthens and maintains flexibility in the heart and blood vessels. This can be seen on ultrasound taken during practice— the heart changes shape in response to different postures. Yet because yoga is less coronary-intensive than other exercise regimes, less lactic acid builds up in the muscles and this in turn avoids fatiguing the circulatory and skeletal systems. Backbends develop the cardiac sphincter as well as the anterior and lateral walls of the heart so blood flow remains strong. Furthermore inversions and restorative postures give gravity a chance to work out the blood vessels in a new way, reducing formation of varicose veins, for example, and increasing circulation to the brain.

Endocrine System

The endocrine system monitors and produces hormonal secretions that regulate body activities. Largely controlled by glands, this system is centred in two areas: the thymus in the mid-sternal area and the thyroid in the neck. When functioning well, this system creates a healthy balance (homeostasis) within the body, maintaining the strength of the immune system and increasing resistance to illness. The act of stretching elongates both muscles, organs and glands, flattening and squeezing out venous blood, leaving them ready to accept a complete dose of freshly oxygenated blood. Thus asanas which affect the endocrine glands (shoulder stands or backbends) maintain them at full vitality.

HUMAN MIND AND ROLE OF YOGA IN MENTAL HEALTH

Our understanding of the human mind and behaviour requires multiple approaches and involves a variety of academic disciplines. This article comes mainly from psychology and associated disciplines with approaches ranging from the biological and genetic to the social and cultural. Each has something to offer our understanding, and none in itself is complete. Rather, we get the best understanding of mind and behaviour by looking at different approaches together.

The contents in this section give a brief glimpse of psychologically oriented studies contributing to our understanding of the human mind and behaviour. The exploration begins with the evolution of mind. Although we are often aware of how thinking and behaviour develop from childhood through adulthood and into old age, we seldom think of evolutionary forces' influence on mind and behaviour. John Elliott's article introduces us to evolutionary psychology and some insights that can be gleaned from examining how behaviour and thought have evolved with mankind.

Evolutionary psychology focuses on genetic relatedness and its relationship to behaviour but generally does not examine individual genes. However, with rapid progress in the field of genetics, we are now able to examine the role of specific genes as they influence personality and psychological processes. Redford William's discussion of current work investigating gene-environment interaction provides a good background for the manner in which specific genes interact with aspects of environment to influence personality, emotion, and health risk, with a specific focus on genes involved with serotonin. Scientists know that this neurotransmitter plays an important role in mood regulation and in such psychological problems as depression. Genes do not operate in isolation, but their effects vary in different environments.

Although mental processes hold our interest in their own right, current research in the area of health psychology is discovering ways in which mental processes influence not just mental health but physical health as well. The article on emotions and health focuses on how emotions can affect health via physiological responses to various environmental events. Such negative emotions as fear and anger can damage health whereas positive emotions such as optimism have protective effects. A recent Singapore workshop showed the importance of these relationships: teaching people skills for dealing with upsetting situations and building stronger relationships with others can help reduce negative emotions, increase positive emotions, and decrease physiological responses to stress—effects that can lead to improvement in physical health.

The word 'mind', especially in the psychology of the West, is used to signify a general operation of the psyche inside, including understanding, willing and feeling. The word 'mind' is a general term in Western psychology, but in the psychology of Yoga, a more detailed analysis has been made. 'Mind' is not a proper English translation of what the Yoga calls 'Chitta', especially in the system of Patanjali. The entire mind-stuff is called Chitta. It is better to use the word 'psyche' instead of the word 'mind', because the former denotes a larger composite structure than the single function indicated by the word 'mind'. Mind is that which thinks in an indeterminate manner; the intellect is that which thinks in a determinate manner; the ego is that which asserts the individuality of one's own self. There are other functions of the psyche such as memory, often associated with the subconscious level. It is impossible for anyone to be aware that something is outside, unless there is an isolated thinking or an individualising principle, known in the Vedanta psychology as the Antahkarana, and in the Yoga psychology of Patanjali as Chitta. "Antahkarana" is a Sanskrit term, which literally translated into English, would mean, "the internal organ". That is perhaps the best way we can put it in English. The internal organ, by which we cognise or perceive things outside, is the Antahkarana. The same thing is called Chitta in Yoga psychology. We need not pay much attention to the peculiar distinguishing factors or features or connotations associated with these words in the different schools of thought. But, it is important to remember that a psychic function inwardly as an individualising principle is necessary in order to assert that the world is outside or that anything is outside.

As discussed already things are not really outside. As such, our persistence that things are outside poses a big mystery. Obviously, the functions of the mind are a blunder. What we call the mind is clearly a miscalculated affirmation. A terrible catastrophe has befallen us in the shape of our persisting in an error which is contrary to the truths of the universe. If the universe or the world is not really outside us, and if we are not seeing anything; but seeing externality, we are surely in a world of blunders. We are perpetually committing mistakes after mistakes, with the result that our entire life may be regarded as a heap or a mountain of mistakes, all mistakes being the consequences of our original self-affirmation called variously as the mind, the Chitta, and the Antahkarana. It is easy enough to appreciate why the mind is to be controlled.

The mind is to be controlled, because it is the essence of mischief-making, because it is the root cause of all the troubles in life. The mind is the central mischief in the individual personality. It is the great dacoit, as Acharya Sankara calls it, the thief who robs us of all wealth and makes us paupers, looking beggarly in the eyes of all people. Why should the mind be controlled? Why should there be a need felt to restrain the Antahkarana? Because the mind is the principle of mistakenly asserting the existence of an externality which is really not there. The nature of things is such that the mind's functions, as they are being carried on now, are uncalled for, unwarranted, and thoroughly erroneous. We do not see things as they are, and therefore, we cannot act also correctly, inasmuch as action is preceded by thought, and thought is a mistaken movement of ourselves.

Now comes Yoga with a great message to us. Our life being a movement in the wrong direction, landing us in repeated problems and rebirths, it is necessary to station ourselves in the true position in which we essentially are, and not lose our own selves. Loss of self is the greatest of losses. We have lost ourselves in imagining that we are not the thing that we actually are in relation to the nature of the universe. We have lost ourselves in imagining that we are isolated persons—men, women and children and many other things—in relation to the nature of the universe. In order that we may be freed from this turmoil or sorrow called Samsara, or life in this empirical world, Yoga comes as a rescue, as a message of hope and solace, telling us that there is no hope for humanity, that there is no chance of peace prevailing anywhere, if self-restraint is not going to be the law of life. Self-restraint, in a way, is the same as mind restraint, because we are practically the same as the mind. We do not make much of a difference between self restraint and restraint of the mind. Because, for us Jivas, empirical individuals the mind itself is the sorrow. What we are, as we appear now, is just the mind operating.

The need for self-control or control of the mind arises on account of the need for perfection which is the goal of everyone. We do not wish to be suffering like this. Our final ambition, aspiration or desire is redress of grief and attainment of freedom which we have not seen with our eyes in this world. None has seen really what freedom is. Everyone is bound in one way or the other. When we imagine that we have got out of a bondage and entered a state of freedom, actually we have entered into another kind of bondage in the name of freedom, a fact which we will realise sometime later. There is no such thing as real freedom in this world, because freedom is the same as attunement with the state of ultimate perfection, or at least, a degree of perfection. If we are far away from even the least percentage of what perfection can be, and our ideals and ideologies in life pursue a phantasm, we cannot hope to have peace in this world by any amount of technological progress. People today are carried away by gadgets and instruments, and researches in the field of externalised technology. This is not an achievement. If by science it is meant the logical knowledge of the nature of things, science is wonderful: it is unavoidable in life. But, if by science is meant technological inventions, setting up of factories and industrial organisation, science is a bane on human life. It will not help us, because it carries us further away from the centre of reality, and compels us to affirm more and more that the world is outside us, rather than the fact that we are inseparable from the world.

Yoga plays a greater role in the management of mental health. The science of Yoga, is a psychology of a philosophical nature. The very introduction of the system of Yoga by Patanjali is by way of an instruction that the mind has to be controlled—*Yogas chitta-vritti-nirodhah.* Patanjali does not go into the details of the philosophical background of the necessity to control the mind, the background that comes in Samkhya and Vedanta. Yoga is control of the mind, restraint of the mind-stuff. Yoga is *Chitta-vritti-nirodhah.* The moment we hear this, we begin to get excited. Yoga is control of the mind. Therefore, we have to control ourselves. We begin to close our eyes, hold our nose, and become nervous and tense in our system! That is an unfortunate result that often follows from an over-enthusiasm, emotionally aroused in ourselves by hearing the very word Yoga. We should not be stirred up into an emotion, just because we listen to the word Yoga mentioned by somebody. A calm and sober understanding is Yoga. Yoga is not emotion. It is not stirring oneself into any kind of made-up or artificial individuality.

Now we know what 'union' actually means in the language of Yoga proper. It is a complete transcendence of our finitude. A separatist tendency persists in us, and Yoga is nothing but overcoming the barriers of this individuality by entering into the oceanic expanse of our true nature, which is also the nature of everybody. When the mind is restrained in this manner, *Chitta-vritti-nirodhah* is affected. This false feeling that we are different from others, that things are constituted of isolated particularities, leaves us; and we get established in our essential nature, which is the community of existence in all things, and not an isolated individuality. This establishment of one's own self in one's own true nature, in universal character, is the aim of Yoga.

When the person who has restrained the mind-stuff has realised that the things are not outside himself, the object ceases to be, and with it, the inside also goes. So, no more is there such a thing as subjectivity or individuality for that person. It does not exist anymore. Thus from the restraint of the mind or the control of the mind follows a re-installation of one's own self in one's own true nature. All negative emotions can be eliminated through various practices of Yoga. Practice of Yoga brings a positive attitude in life.

V

Yoga and Health Care

CONCEPT OF DISEASE AND HEALTH IN YOGA

In common usage, a disease is any abnormal condition of the body or mind that causes discomfort or dysfunction. A disease or medical condition is an abnormal condition of an organism that impairs bodily functions, associated with specific symptoms and signs. It may be caused by external factors, such as infectious disease, or it may be caused by internal dysfunctions, such as autoimmune diseases.

In humans, "disease" is often used more broadly to refer to any condition that causes pain, dysfunction, distress, social problems, and/or death to the person afflicted or similar problems for those in contact with the person. In this broader sense, it sometimes includes injuries, disabilities, disorders, syndromes, infections, isolated symptoms, deviant behaviours, and atypical variations of structure and function, while in other contexts and for other purposes these may be considered distinguishable categories.

According to yoga philosophy there are five sheaths of human existence, first and innermost is physical body, second is vital body known as *Prana* through which vital energy flows throughout the *nadis*. The third sheath is mind, which is the seat of emotions and thoughts while the fourth sheath is our knowledge termed as intellect. Last and outermost sheath is known as Bliss/ Soul which includes universal consciousness.

Yogic principle says—imbalance of energy produces disease. Our soul is a part of supreme consciousness and is pure. The fourth and fifth sheath is permeated by a universal consciousness and is not disturbed by our actions/ thinking. When a person is truly healthy, the positive energy in the highest sheath percolates freely to lower ones and brings total harmony to all faculties. However, imbalances in first three sheaths can block free flow of energy. This imbalance in lower sheaths is the cause of diseases.

The root cause of stress induced ailments is the amplified likes and dislikes at the *Manomaya kosa* which results in distressful emotional surges called

'Aadhi'. The life style gets disturbed because of long standing uncontrolled surges of stressful reactions like intense desire (Kama), anger (Krodha), fear (Bhaya), jealousy (Matsarya), etc. These agitations cause violent fluctuations in the flow of prana in the 'naadis' which are said to be the channels distributed all over the body through their branching system.

Each and every cell in the body, requires the right quota of its pranic energy to carry on its biochemical processes in an efficient way. The example is that of uninterrupted power supply necessary for every electrical gadget in right quantities. Just as these equipments would fail if there is any irregularity in the power supply, human organ systems fail to function if they do not get the right quantum of *prana*. Thus the disturbances in the *Manomaya kosa* percolate into physical body (Annamaya Kosa) through disturbed prana flows. Hence the management of these stress induced ailments should correct imbalances at all these levels. Yoga techniques are offered to correct the imbalances through a set of yoga practices which we have termed as integrated approach of yoga therapy. These are practised to correct the problem at various levels.

Yoga considers that most diseases are due to insufficient life force, either in the body as a whole, or a blockage of life force to one part of the body. This leads to a lowered body resistance or immunity to disease. Those practicing yoga have learned many centuries ago that most diseases are due to reduced immunity. Medical science is gradually coming to the same conclusion.

When the whole body has lowered life force, the result is a lowered vitality level, poor health and susceptibility to infection. No infections would occur if the body's life force is high enough to fight off the infection. Pathogens (bacteria, viruses and so on) are a normal part of life and will only cause trouble when the body's resistance is too low to keep them in check. The best way to increase the general life force of the body is by good nutrition, sufficient deep steep, a positive mental attitude and yoga.

A blockage of life force to one part of the body, such as the thyroid gland, is usually caused by a slight misalignment of a vertebra which impinges on the nerve that travels to that particular organ. This causes an interference to the life force (nerve impulses) to the organ. As a result, the organ does not function at its optimum level. If the spinal misalignment is not corrected, the organ may develop pathology. It is much more difficult to correct at this stage.

The ancient yogis were well aware of the importance of the spine in relation to disease, since most of their *asanas* or postures were designed to make the spine more flexible to prevent spinal misalignments. Some of the *asanas* will even correct minor spinal misalignments. The spine is so important for a high vitality level, good health and the correction of many health conditions that a whole science of healing has been developed to correct spinal misalignments. In fact, chiropractic is now the second largest fastest growing healing profession after medicine.

IMPORTANCE OF YOGIC PRACTICES FOR COMMON MAN

In daily life, yoga helps the person to attain a relaxed state of mind. It provides him/her with vitality, vigor and zest to carry out his/her life. All negative blocks in the mind are removed. The body is cleansed of all the impurities and toxins.

Personal power is enhanced by the practice of yoga. One learns to identify their own inner resources and draw upon the energy needed from their own inner sources. It helps one to increase his or her awareness, i.e. self-awareness. It helps in attention, focus and concentration.

The whole science of yoga has one view in common—to gain health, personal power, to develop knowledge and attain peace of mind. It also reduces stress and tension in the physical body, and activates the parasympathetic nervous system.

Several studies have shown that yoga significantly improves the condition of bronchial asthmatics, even including the patients who were childhood asthmatics. Many subjects eventually reduced or eliminated their need for medication. Yoga has been shown to significantly decrease hyperglycemia in non-insulin dependent diabetics.

Yoga has been shown to significantly improve mental and physical energy levels and alertness as compared to relaxation exercises and visualisation.

One study showed that yoga resulted in a gradual, significant decrease in body weight. In addition there was an increase in alpha wave activity in parts of the brain which corresponds to an increase in calmness. Yoga has been shown to produce a significant increase in serum LDH levels (the enzyme which provides energy to contracting muscles during exercise). Other studies have shown that yoga can help conditions of arthritis, arteriosclerosis, chronic fatigue, varicose veins, and heart ailments. Specific yoga breathing postures and breathing exercises have been led to significant improvements in patients with Obsessive-Compulsive Disorder (OCD).

Yoga stretches and tones the muscles and joints; it has a positive effect on the entire skeletal system including the spine, and has a positive effect on all the organs, glands, and nerves. Many of the yogic postures and breathing exercises bring much needed blood and oxygen to bodily tissues and organs which speeds the healing of the practitioner. Releasing built up physical and emotional tension slowly liberates vast resources of energy. Finally, and not to be underestimated in importance, a regular yoga practice can gradually and significantly increase a person's sense of self-acceptance and inner peace.

Yoga's primary emphasis is upon general well-being. Although yoga has been shown to be beneficial in a variety of conditions, it is not considered a therapy for specific illnesses. Rather, yoga employs a broad holistic approach that focuses on teaching people a new lifestyle, way of thinking, and way of being in the world. In the process, however, it is also found to bring a myriad of healing effects. By attending to practices for improving, regaining or retaining general good health, a person is likely to find that some of his/her more specific difficulties tend to disappear. Many of the healing effects of yoga are clinically verified. One of the most important benefits of yoga is its application in relieving stress, fatigue, invigoration and vitality and its anti-aging properties and its application for relaxation therapy.

As man is a physical, mental and spiritual being, yoga helps to promote a balanced development of all the three. Physical exercises, aerobics and other forms of exercises assure welfare only to the physical body, and not to the spiritual body or the astral body.

Yogic exercises help to promote an all-round well being in an individual. They help to recharge the body with cosmic energy. This helps to attain perfect equilibrium and harmony. Yoga helps the aspirant to channelise and harness the cosmic energy for self-healing. Consequently, it produces peace and positive feelings in the mind of the aspirant. It rejuvenates and energizes the body. Development and healing is brought about from within. Regular practice of Asanas, pranayama and meditation can help such diverse ailments such as diabetes, blood pressure, digestive disorders, arthritis, arteriosclerosis, chronic fatigue, asthma, varicose veins and heart conditions. Laboratory tests have proved a yogi's increased abilities of consciously controlling autonomic or involuntary functions, such as temperature, heart-beat and blood pressure. Research into the effects of yogic practices on HIV is currently underway with promising results.

According to medical scientists, yoga therapy is successful because of the balance created in the nervous and endocrine systems which directly influences all the other systems and organs of the body. Yoga acts both as a curative and preventive therapy. The very essence of yoga lies in attaining mental peace, improved concentration powers, a relaxed state of living and harmony in relationships.

Recomended Practices for Common Man

The recomended practices for them are:

Asanas: Sandhi sanḉhalana practices (with breath awareness) Tadasana, Tiryaktadasana and Katiḉhakrasana (each 5 rounds) Surya Namaskar (2-5 rounds), Śavasana 15 minutes, Halasana (each 5 minutes.) Pasḉhimottanasana, Dhanurasana, Padmasana, Siddhasana, Ardhamatsyendrasana and Śavasana (again 5 minutes.)

Pranayamas: Nadi śodhan, Bhastrika, Śītali ad Bhramari.

Kryas: Kapalbhati daily (25 strokes) Jal Neti and Vaman (once a week) Loghū Śankha praksalana (once a month)

Special Practices: Yoga nidra, So-ham Sadhana, Gayatri Mantra Japa.

Other Recommendation: Adopt a regular schedule with Yogic practices as well as try to be stress free.

The aspirant should go through a holistic practice of yoga. Which includes not only Asana or Pranayama, but the cleansing (Śatkarma) and meditation. Asana and Pranayama work on physical and mental level only. Cleansing removes the *Mal* (The waste of body and mind); which is necessary for all. Practice of meditation balances one emotionally and spiritually. Only then, one can get benefited through Yoga.

Physiologically and psychologically the regular practitioner of Yoga will be able to enjoy better sleep, a happier disposition, a clearer and calmer mind. One can learn how to build up the health and protect himself against colds, fevers, constipation, headaches, fatigue, and other troubles. He will know what to do in order to remain youthful, vital and alert, regardless of the calendar-age; how to lose or gain weight; how to get rid of premature wrinkles, and keep a smooth skin and clear complexion.

Spiritualy through regular practice of yoga, we become aware of the interconnectedness between our emotional, mental and physical levels. Gradually this awareness leads to an understanding of the more subtle areas of existence. The ultimate goal of yoga is to make it possible for you to be able to fuse together the gross material (annamaya), physical (pranamaya), mental (manomaya), intellectual (vijnanamaya) and spiritual (anandamaya) levels within.

YOGIC MANAGEMENT OF COMMON DISORDERS

Each person who desires peace for the whole world is praise worthy. But one cannot achieve the goal only by desiring it. Every mother wants her child to be healthy, wealthy and wise, but how many of them can make it possible? Every student and every player wants to make best presentation, but how many gets success? It is good to desire the best, but only that person can get success, whose devotion is deep and longstanding. When a mother understands the laws of health and growth and creates the environment accordingly, definitely her child becomes healthy. When a player properly understands the rules and regulations of the game and starts playing accordingly, he gets success definitely. The same rule applies to the field of Yoga.

Along with the desire of peace it requires deep devotion also. Who will do such hard work? Which type of devotion it will be? Which types of obstacles are there and how to overcome it? All these questions require attention.

Resources and intellectual development have been taking place in last few decades. People attracted by this development, stated thinking that by getting education and comforts, they can achieve the peace. But within some period they realize that it is their misconception. It can be seen that most rich and educated persons problems of illness and depression. It is being observed that there is no person without having stress, sorrow and disturbed mental state. All the crime, crises and terrorism are being channelised through them, who are educated and have sufficient resources. In the absence of these, it is impossible to plan these things. Through this study it can be said that peace cannot be achieved through resources and education. The source of peace is different from these. Our seers saints and the world famous thinkers have described the source of peace and the clue to their achievements is the regular practice of Yoga only.

Yoga is a comprehensive and precisely live tuned process for uniting the individual consciousness with the omnipresent cosmic consciousness. Understanding the spiritual nature and philosophy of yoga is certainly more important than its gross applications. It is a total science of strengthening and improving the physical, mental, and spiritual state of being.

Hypertension and its Yogic Managenment

Hypertension is an important and a common ailment and risk factor considerable morbidity and mortality not only in the industrialized world but also in the developing countries. The problem of hypertension can be truly considered as pandemic. An increased pressure blood results from the damming up of blood behind constricted arterioles, upsetting the balance of heart and its vessels.

Tension is the central theme of all mind related diseases. This tension is due to the strain of life that an individual carries. It is well established that the brain with its known centers for sensory intellectual and emotional tensions play the main role in maintaining by releasing required amount of neurohumors and hormones. Any disorder of this homeostatic factor would ultimately lead to the development of tension related therapies which have been unable to cure or prevent hypertension.

Now a days the problem of the circulatory system has become common. Increased blood pressure may cause many dangerous diseases. Prolonged stress is the root cause of this disorder. This pressure increases when the arteries become stiff and hard. Heredity, aging, smoking, high cholesterol diet and sedentary lifestyle are the other causes of this disease.

To relax the stiffness of the arteries, decrease the cholesterol level from blood and release the stress are the aims of yoga.

Recommendations

Practices recommended for those suffering from this disease are:

Āsanas: (Sandhi-Sanchalan) with breath awareness Tādāsana, Tiryaktādāsana, Katichakrāsana (slowly 5 rounds) Śavāsana (15 minutes). Sarpāsana and Makarāsana.

Prānāyāma: Nādiśodhan, Ujjai, Śītali and Bhrāmari (5 rounds).

Kryās: Kapālbhāti (moderate way 15-25 strokes) Jal neti (daily).

Precautions: Hard practices should not be attempted without a good instructor, whenever (during the practice) you feel exertion go into śavasana.

Other Recommendations: Walk slowly for a few minutes, try to be stress free. Take a cholesterol free diet and leave addictions if any.

Heart Disease and Yoga

Heart and the circulatory system are the most complicated part of human body.

Angina pectoris, atherosclerosis, cardiac failure and hypertension etc. are the common problems with heart. Although they are known as separate problems they all are interrelated to each other.

The increased cholesterol and sugar in the blood while circulating through the arteries make them stiff and constricted and circulation becomes difficult. Cardiac work load becomes high and the prolonged stage of situation makes the heart exerted. All the irregularities start from this stage. It begins with hypertension and heart pain which later becomes atherosclerosis, and thus results in cardiac failure.

Yogic Principle: For a heart patient it is a must that they've to be very careful. Negligence may be dangerous. Pranayama should be more emphasized here, than Asana because strain and more efforts should be avoided. The aim of yoga is to regulate the circulation and reduce the cholesterol and sugar from the blood.

Recommendations

Practices recommended for them are:

Āsanas: Sandhi Sanchālan (with breath awareness) for proper blood circulation, Tādāsana, Tiryaktādāsana, Katichakrāsana (5 rounds each) Śavāsana (15 minutes), PragyāYoga Vyāyama (1-2 rounds slowly), Again Śavāsana

Prānāyāmas: Nādiśodhan (without retention) Śītali, Ujjai and Bhrāmari (7 rounds each).

Kryās: Kapālbhāti (10-25 strokes daily) Jal neti (daily).

Special: Yoga nidrā So-ham Sādhnā, Gāyatri Mantra Japa.

Precautions: Do not try strenuous exercises or yogic asanas and whenever you feel exertion, practices śavāsana.

Other Recommendations: Try to be stress free. Take cholesterol less diet, and stop all addictions. Make a positive attitude towards life. For relief from emotional imbalance, pray God and get devoted.

Diabetes Mellitus and Yoga

Diabetes is caused by the increased sugar level in blood in the body. It represents a cluster of metabolic diseases characterized by high levels of blood glucose (hyperglycemia). This may be as a result of defects in insulin secretion, insulin action or both. Insulin is a hormone secreted by beta cells of islets of langerhans, situated in pancreas. The glucagons produced by alfa cells have anti-insulin action. Both in unison keep a constant glucose level in the blood. Insulin also acts as gate-keeper, where, only in its presence can the blood glucose enter the body cells and provide fuel and energy to work. In diabetes, the cellular fuel is thus compromised, while excess of glucose remains in the circulation.

The pancreas (ductless gland) either slows the secretion of insulin or stops the secretion. It can be diagnosed by presence poly-urea and late recovery of wounds. Diabetes is mainly of two types. Juvenile which is mainly found in the children and the second Maturity Onset Diabetes-which comes during aging. Main cause of Juvenile is heredity; there are also other causes. Maturity On set diabetes is a decaying process and comes due to aging, stress and Sedentary life style and too much consumption of sweets and sugar products.

Regular practice of yoga does reduce blood sugar levels, blood pressure, weight, and rate of progression of complications, and the severity of the complications as well. The symptoms are also reduced to a great extent, so are number of diabetes related hospital admissions. The quality of life questionnaires do reveal a remarkable improvement in the scores. These finding are uniform for all those who are trying to find effect of yoga on diabetes.

Yogic Principle: The aim of Yogic practices are to regulate the pancreas and reduce the sugar level from the body. The patients may also suffer from obesity and so practices should be gentle and then increased gradually.

How does Yoga work? (Possible mechanisms)

Glucagons secretion is enhanced by stress. Yoga effectively reduces stress, thus reducing glucagons and possibly improving insulin action. Weight loss induced by yoga is a well accepted mechanism.

Muscular relaxation, development and improved blood supply to muscles might enhance insulin receptor expression on muscles causing increased glucose uptake by muscles and thus reducing blood sugar. Blood pressure plays a great role in development of diabetic and related complications, which is proven to be benefited by yoga. The same holds true for increased cholesterol levels.

Yoga reduces adrenaline, noradrenalin and cortisol in blood, which are termed as 'stress hormones'. This is a likely mechanism of improvement in insulin action. Many yogic postures do produce stretch on the pancreas, which is likely to stimulate the pancreatic function.

Recommendations

Practices recommended for them are:

Āsanas: Tādāsana, Tiryaktādāsana, Katicharkrāsana (5 rounds each) Surya Namaskār (3-7 rounds) Śavāsana (10 minutes). Udar Sanchālan practices, Śaktibandha practices, Paschimottānāsana, or Saśānkāsana, Dhanurāsana or

Bhujangāsana, Ardha matsyendrāsana or Vakrāsana, Halāsana or Ardhahalāsana Sarvāngāsana or Viprītkarnī, Śavāsana (again 10 minutes).

Prānāyāma: Bhastrikā, Nādiśodhan, Śītali, Bhrāmari (5 each).

Kṛyās: Kapālbhāti (30-100 strokes), Jal neti and Vaman (twice a week) Laghū Samkha Prakśālana (once a week).

Special: Yoga nidrā and So-ham sādhanā.

Precautions: If suffering from hypertension and heart disease, first control them with the given practices for them.

Other Recommendations: Sit in Vajrāsana after every meal, walk fast for a few kilometers daily.

Asthma and Yoga

Respiration is the process through which we supply oxygen as per the requirement of each and every cell of our body. In the condition of less oxygen supply, the cells start degenerating and body becomes weak.

Asthma is a complicated disorder of our respiratory system. The secretion of mucous interrupts the respiration. Bronchial spasm makes a feeling of breathlessness and later on thick mucous recetion with coughing. After a long time complication increases and sufferer becomes weaker. The main cause is allergens but psychological and other causes like cold and heredity are also common. Any age group can be affected by this disorder.

Yogic Principle: Patients generally have problems with breathing. Due to less oxygen intake and, less prāna intake, some becomes weak. Yogic practices aim at regeneration of the pranic energy in the body, at the same time, removal of extra secretion of mucous.

Yogic Asanas and Pranayamas in combination not only regulate the breathing pattern; it also improves the lungs functioning as well. With the forceful pumping of lungs the pulmonary ventilation improves. Proper oxygen supply improves metabolic rate. Hence proper absorption and assimilation of food improves the vitality as well the immunity of the body.

Recommendations

Practices recommended for them are:

Āsanas: Tādāsana, Tiryaktādāsana, Kati chakrāsana, Marjāriāsana (5 rounds' each), Saśānk bhujangāsana (according to strength) Śavāsana (10 minutes), Surya Namaskār (slowly 1 to 5 rounds), Makarāsana, Bhujangāsana, Dhanurāsana, Gomukhāsana, Śavāsana (again).

Prānāyāma: Nādiśodhan (5 rounds), Bhastrikā, Suryabhedan (7 each).

Kṛyās: Kapālbhāti (20-100 strokes according to strength) Jal Neti and Kunjal (thrice a week).

Special Practices: So-ham sādhanā, Yoga nidrā.

Other Recommendations: Fasting in a week should be observed. Rice, sweets and dairy products should be avoided.

Obesity and Yoga

It is a common disorder today. Women are more prone to get obese than men. For the males total height in inches minus four Kgms and for females total height in inches six Kgms is the ideal body weight. If a male having 5 feet 6 inches height, his weight 62 Kgms is ideal whereas for the same height in females, 60 Kgms will be ideal. More or less 5 kgms can be considered as normal. More than that the person is recognized as obese.

Obesity can be seen in the children in the present time. Its two main causes are, thyroid disorder and the heredity.

The problem of obesity has been observed in females after their first delivery. The causes are Sedentary life style and unlimited diet. Generally obesity is due to little body movements. Psychologists consider it a stress related disorder. Whereas Yoga says it is due to 'Tamas' in life.

Yogic Principle: It is wrong to think that obesity will be cured with quick practices. Because obese patients get tired easily, so they should adopt the simple practices, later on with the time body will become stronger and the practices will be increased.

Recommendations

Practices recommended for them:

Āsanas: Tādāsana, Tiryaktādāsana, Kati Chakrāsana, Marjariāsana (5 round' each), Saśānk bhujangāsana (according to strength) Śavāsana (10 minutes), Surya Namaskār (slowly 1 to 5 rounds), Makarāsana, Bhujangāsana, Dhanurāsana, Gomukhāsana, Śavāsana (again).

Prānāyāma: Nādiśodhan, Bhastrikā, Suryabhedan, Bhrāmari (5 rounds each)

Kṛyās: Kapālbhāti (25-100 strokes daily) Kunjal (once a week), Laghū. sankhaprakśālana (once a week).

Special Practice: Yoga nidrā.

Spinal Problem and Yoga

The disorder of the spine like spondylitis and backache are commonly observed. In both states the disorder symptoms start with simple pain in particular area. The basic cause is vertebral degeneration. It may be due to wrong posture or rupture.

Females mostly have the lower back pain because they generally work with forward bending where as cervical spondylitis has been seen in males because of work on computer and use of high pillows. Sometimes vertebrae can be observed to be a little bit displaced.

Yogic Principle: Here, yoga aims to correct the wrong posture as well as stop degeneration of the system. At the same time pranic flow improves and the body wastes get eliminated.

Recommendations

Practices recommended for them are:

Āsanas: Sandhi Sanchālan practices (except Neck exercises) Mārjariāsana, Makarāsana, Bhujangāsana, Ardha śalabhāsana, Vajrāsana, Sarpāsana, Pragyā yoga vyāyām (if possible), Śavāsana (10-15 minutes)

Prāṇāyāmas: Nādi śodhan, Ujjai, Bhrāmari (5 each).

Kryās: Kapālbhāti (25-50 strokes daily), Jal neti, Vaman (once a week), Laghū sankhaprakśālana (once a week).

Other recommendations: Try to keep the intestine clear because pain will increase with constipation.

Precautions: During the acute pain get rest, do not strain.

ARTHRITIS AND YOGA

Arthritis is mainly the joint problem. Ayurveda consider it as Vata disorder and the modern science suggests that the decaying of synovial fluid between the gaps of bones is the main cause of this disorder. The problem is caused by sedentary life style and secondly by the consumption of taking of Vata dominated food. Aging and degenerations are the other causes.

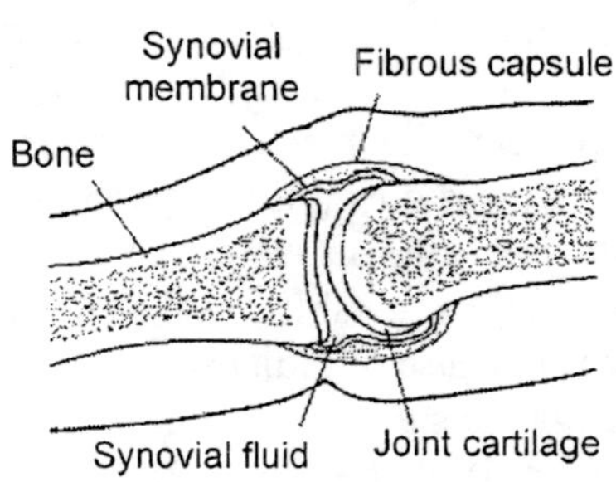

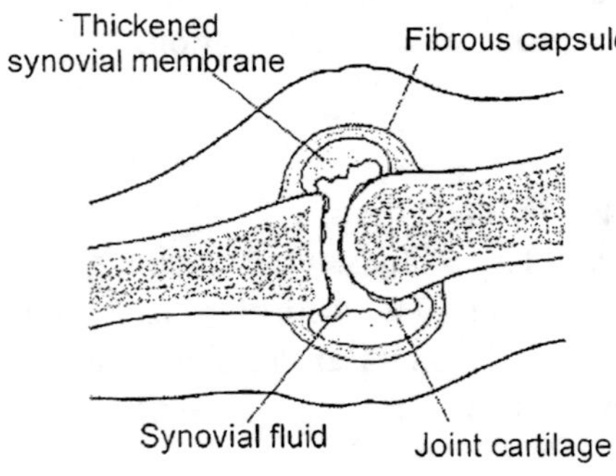

For the proper movements of joints the thing which is needed is synovial fluid; its insufficiency and deposition of waste in them create pain and stiffness. It is found in every age group with different symptoms in which Gout and Reumatoid Arthritis are common, but causes are different.

Yogic Principle: Yoga aims at removal of the waste from the joints and to fulfill the insufficiency of synovial fluid and also try to activate the blocked prānic flow.

Recommendations

Practices recommended for them are:

Āsanas: Sandhi Sanchālan practices, Udar sanchālana practices, Śavāsana (10 minutes), Pragyāyoga Vyāyāma or Surya namaskār (if possible) Vajrāsana (if possible).

Prānāyāma: Nādi śodhan, Bhastrikā, Bhrāmari (5 each).

Kryās: Neti, Vaman, Laghū sankhaprakśālana (once a week), Kapālbhāti (10-50 strokes).

Special: Yoga nidrā, So-ham sādhanā Gāyatri Mantra.

Other Recommendations: Walk for small distances regularly, avoid dairy products. Adopt green leafy vegetables in meals.

Digestive Disorder and Yoga

Digestive system is one of the functional and important systems of the body. Here the macro molecules are converted into micro molecules and give nutrition and energy to the whole body. Problem of this system ultimately brings imbalance in the total physiology. Constipation and indigestion are two main disorders.

Indigestion is the problem of stomach where the meal taken is not easily to digested and hunger becomes down. Constipation is the disorder of large intestine where after absorption, the defecation becomes difficult. Less use of water and lack of fibres, leafy vegetable are the root cause of constipation where as rich diet is the root cause of indigestion.

Yogic Principle: Yoga aims to change the Sedentary life style, activate the digestive fire (Jatharāgni) at the same time; it aims at activating the abdominal muscles for proper digestive secretion.

Recommendations

Practices recommended for them are:

Āsanas: Tādāsana, Tiryaktādāsana, Katichakrāsana, Suryanamaskār (5 rounds each) Śavāsana (10 minutes) Vajrāsana, Mārjariāsana, Paśimottanāsana, Halāsana, Dhanurāsana or bhujangāsana, Śavāsana (again).

Prānāyāmas: Nādiśodhan, Bhrāmari (5 each).

Kṛyas: Kapālbhāti (30-100 strokes daily), Neti, Vaman and laghū śankhpraksālana (once a week), Nauli or Agnisārkṛyā (Three rounds daily).

Special Practice: So-Ham sādhanā.

Other Recommendations: Take 4-6 glasses of water before defecation in the morning. Walk for a small distance fast. Give up the habit of always chewing something. Adopt vegetarian diet with more starch.

Precautions: Persons who've hypertension, heart disease and acute constipation problems should not indulge in rigorous practice of yoga.

VI

Role of Yoga for Healthy Lifestyle

HEALTHY LIFE STYLE AND ITS IMPORTANCE IN HEALTHY LIVING

Health is a natural facet of liveliness—both by definition and realization. The ancient Indians had attributed the secret of ***"jivem shardah shatam"***—hundred years of vigorous, healthy, happy and creative life—to the total harmony of the mode of living with the Nature and the spiritual inheritance of life.

Lifestyle plays an important role in healthy living. Overall good health comes from strict and consistent attention to what we put in our bodies and what we do to maintain our physical fitness. When it comes to our diet, we all understand the important elements of maintaining health; a commitment to eating natural, whole foods and avoiding foods high in fat. But physical fitness, more than anything, helps protect our body from diseases and keeps us strong and healthy well into the future.

How to have a healthy life? An effective fitness routine includes exercise that works with our current health and lifestyle. If you are currently sedentary, begin a fitness routine very slowly—incorporating a small amount of exercise into your daily schedule and increasing it as your strength and conditioning increase. Walking is a wonderful exercise that positively impacts all areas of your body and can be easily done by anyone. Start walking a little bit each day and increase your speed and distance as you feel stronger.

In sociology, a lifestyle is the way a person lives. Sedentary lifestyle is the big risk factor in common disorders. Sedentary lifestyle is a medical term used to denote a type of lifestyle with no or irregular physical activity. A person who lives a sedentary lifestyle may colloquially be known as a couch potato. It is commonly found in both the developed and developing world. Sedentary activities include sitting, reading, watching television and computer use for much of the day with little or no vigorous physical exercise. A sedentary lifestyle can contribute to many preventable causes of death.

A sedentary lifestyle is a way of living in which a person does not engage in sufficient physical activity for what is generally considered healthy living.

It is marked by prolonged period of sitting, whether it is around the TV or the computer screen or anything else. People living a sedentary lifestyle overlook physical activity and are involved in activities that rarely require any amount of physical stress. According to a new study, following a sedentary lifestyle can be more dangerous for your health than smoking. There is a lot of research conducted on the effects of sedentary lifestyle on an individual across the globe. The findings of these researches can be mentioned as follows:

The major effect of a sedentary lifestyle can be seen on the size of your trousers. Because you are ingesting a lot of calories and not really burning any of them, these calories are deposited in your body as excess fat. And this is just the beginning of the problems. Your heart must get a proper supply of blood from the blood vessels (coronary arteries) in order to keep functioning efficiently. Leading a sedentary lifestyle can slow the blood circulation and your blood vessels can get stiff and blocked. In serious cases, this can lead to arteriosclerosis and cardiac arrest. According to a study, lack of physical activity in your middle age can increase your risk of dying from heart disease by 52 percent in men and 28 percent in women. Regular exercise helps in regulating the blood glucose levels. According to study conducted by researchers at Duke University Medical Center, intensive exercise can significantly improve the body's ability to control blood sugar levels. The lack of exercise results in increased blood sugar levels putting excess stress on your pancreas (which secretes the hormone Insulin). This increases your chances of getting type 2 diabetes.

Decreased activity increases the risk of developing certain types of cancers such as breast cancer, colon cancer, and other types of malignant tumors. According to a study carried out by the University of Hong Kong, physical inactivity can increase the risk of dying from cancer by 45 percent in men and 28 percent in women. The prolonged inactivity causes your bones to lose their strength as they are no longer challenged to support your body structure. Arthritis and Osteoporosis, which cause the bones to become brittle and weak, can be brought on through an inactive lifestyle.

Your muscles are like car batteries. They need to be run on a regular basis to make sure that the car is working. The more sedentary lifestyle you have the lesser muscles you are likely to posses. The less muscles you posses the lesser is your ability to carry out your day-to-day tasks. Being a couch potato also has a serious effect on your posture and spine health. Sitting all day can shorten and tighten your hip flexors and hamstrings, while making the muscles that support your spine to become weak and stiff.

A sedentary lifestyle doesn't put any physical pressure on the body. Thus the body doesn't feel like taking a rest often which leads to sleeping difficulties and in severe cases can also lead to insomnia. Researchers in Norway found that that people who did not exercise were 14 per cent more likely to develop non-migraine headaches than those who did exercise.

Of course if you have been following a sedentary lifestyle for ages then suddenly getting back to exercise can seem a bit of a daunting task. But if you gradually add low intensity activities like washing your clothes, ironing, walking the dog etc. to your lifestyle and then add high intensity activities like running, cycling etc. you may be well on your way to an active and a healthy lifestyle.

What is a Healthy Lifestyle?

We all know that we should exercise a lot and follow a proper diet programme to keep ourselves healthy. But, to a lot of us it is like grandma's advice—we listen to it and then we forget it and go back to our old ways. We prefer our sedentary lifestyles because it doesn't compel us to do a lot of things. We spend way too much time in front of the television and if that was not enough, we accompany it with a lot of junk food.

How is a Healthy Lifestyle Beneficial?

With the increased understanding of our bodies that we have gained from science over the past few decades, the benefits of a healthy lifestyle are becoming more apparent, along with the reasons as to why we should detoxify the body at least once a year to remove harmful bacteria, and even worms, from our digestive system. For people of all ages, weights, and abilities, the benefits of a healthy lifestyle are endless. But, for now, let's look at eight simple benefits of a healthy lifestyle.

Good Health is not something that you buy from a drug store or a department store, but can be achieved by practicing collective patterns of health-related behaviours based on choices made from available options. Following this logic, if you wish to realize the benefits of a healthy lifestyle, you have to repeat some healthy pattern as a part of your daily or weekly activities, patterns like eating right and exercising. Other benefits include reduced health care costs, reduced illness and injuries, reduced doctors visit, keeps you employed and improved employee/employer relations.

Managing your weight is the key to attaining all the benefits of a Healthy Lifestyle. A weight reduction of just ten percent will significantly reduce risk of heart disease and other obesity-related illnesses. Obesity/overweight is the second leading contributing factor to many childhood diseases such as orthopedic disorders, sleep apnea, type II diabetes mellitus, asthma, high blood pressure and cholesterol, skin disorders, emotional and psychosocial problems, and many more. Weight-bearing exercise such as walking and strength training helps slow the onset of and/or prevent osteoporosis and some research shows that participating in such activities can actually build bone density and begin to reverse the disease. Other benefits are: Weight reduction, reduced tension and stress, improved well-being, Enhanced self-image and self-esteem and improved physical function.

Although drugs alone can often bring cholesterol down to normal levels, diet and exercise provide benefits that drugs don't. They'll lower blood pressure, reduce weight, and lower the risk of developing diabetes. A sedentary lifestyle is a dangerous risk factor for disease. Exercise and a healthy diet helps the body use insulin more efficiently and can help control, alleviate and prevent many diseases. Exercise, cessation of tobacco consumption, eating a high-fiber low-fat diet, controlling body weight, and learning to cope with stress reduce the risk of heart disease.

We all wish a trim and have healthy body for a variety of aesthetic, social and medical reasons. Healthy living is truly the best medicine. In a study conducted by Tufts University at the New England Medical Center, among patients with cardiovascular disease, an exercise programme was shown to significantly reduce LDL cholesterol and other risk factors beyond what's provided by drug therapy. Even modest weight loss can help reduce medical and pharmacy costs, help avoid bariatric surgery, and co-morbidities such as asthma, hypertension, and diabetes.

Wellness is about being comfortable in your space: your body, your attitude, and your environment. A healthy lifestyle can greatly increase a person's longevity. And even though catching something contagious like a cold or flu is sometimes unavoidable, having the wisdom that feeling healthy is a better way to live should have you asking yourself why you are not taking action to live each day as beneficially as possible. The issue with a lot of people nowadays is that they are so busy working and/or taking care of everyone around them, that they neglect their own health and wellness. Make sure your heart is healthy and your bones are strong and Keep it that way to see the benefits of a healthy lifestyle.

The best way to ensure good health is by taking care of yourself. The Care stakes are high but the potential rewards are great-preventing premature death, unnecessary illness, and disability, controlling health care cost, and maintaining a high quality of life into old age. With a healthy lifestyle, you are who you are and you don't have to be self-conscious about those things that you otherwise would be if you didn't care about your lifestyle

With a healthy lifestyle, you have more control of your life as you work with your body against those aspects of living which may work to hold you back if you would let them. With a healthy lifestyle, you have control over your sleep patterns so that you feel generally well rested throughout the day. With a healthy lifestyle, everything works together to help other aspects of your lifestyle make sense and benefit you. Science has proven that healthy weight loss, healthy eating and fitness routines make dramatic improvements in health, and help control common chronic illnesses like high cholesterol, high blood pressure, diabetes, stress, and general lack of stamina.

Another benefit of a healthy lifestyle is a steady flow of stamina and strength; you can perform activities and exercises that will enhance your flexibility. With a healthy lifestyle, you have a balanced and varied diet that provides your body its needed nutrients and energy as well. You have strength to train to help build the muscle that supports the bones and joints, therefore decreasing the risk of falls and fractures. Cardiovascular exercise, also known as aerobic exercise, strengthens the heart muscle, therefore increases the heart's efficiency. As we age, our bones biologically begin to lose mass and strength. Weight-bearing exercise such as walking and strength training helps slow the onset of and/or prevent osteoporosis and some research shows that participating in such activities can actually build bone density and begin to reverse the disease. The good news will be you don't have to get training like an Olympic athlete to enjoy the benefits of a healthy lifestyle. The secret and logic are repeating a chosen healthy pattern as a part of your daily or weekly activities. A healthy lifestyle is a way of life.

YOGA AND HEALTHY LIFESTYLE

Yoga is not only to do with physical postures, breathing exercises or concentrating for a few minutes, as we understand normally, it is a comprehensive and precisely live tuned process of uniting the individual consciousness with the omnipresent cosmic consciousness. Understanding the spiritual nature and philosophy of yoga is certainly more important than its gross applications. Yoga can be understood from the words in Bhagvadgeeta as: *Yogah Karmashu Kaushalam*, i.e. perfection in action is Yoga.

Buddhiyukto jahaatiha ubhe sukrtaduskrte /
Tasmaadyogaaya yujyasva yogah karmasu kaushalam//

One who is endowed with the *samatva buddhi*, sameness of mind, gives up both *punya* and *paapa* here, in this world. Therefore commit yourself to *karma-yoga. Yoga* is discrimination in action. With reference to the results of your actions, there is sameness *samatva* in your response. With reference to action itself, because there is a choice involved, a *karma yogi* always chooses to follow the rules of *dharma*, basic ethics and morality.

Yoga is a lifestyle which regulates one's thought-pattern, character, and behaviour and it reflects in his attitude and personality. It is a total science of strengthening and improving the physical, mental, and spiritual state of being.

If we define Health, it is not only the absence of disease or infirmity, it's a state of complete physical, mental spiritual and social well-being. Health is very nicely defined in ancient Ayurvedic text *Susrut Samhita* in fifteenth chapter verses 41 as:

Samdoshaḥ Samāgnischa Samdhātumalakriyaḥ /
Prassanātmāendriyamanaḥ Swastha Ityabhidhīyate//

Meaning: Only that person is healthy, whose *doshas dhatumal* and *agni* (the basic elements and functional energy streams as per one's natural constitution) are balanced and free from all defects and disorders and whose mind and soul are in perfect harmony.

True health is a state of wholeness where all organ systems of the body function at optimum levels 100 per cent of the time. Health is not simply the absence of sickness. What is the true definition of healthy living? It sounds silly that we need to define healthy living. After all, we know what healthy is and we also know what living is.

According to the World Health Organization (WHO), health is a state of complete physical, mental, and social well-being. Interestingly enough, health is not simply defined as just the absence of disease. The actual definition of healthy living is the steps, actions and strategies one puts in place to achieve optimum health. Healthy living is about taking responsibility and making smart health choices for today and for the future. Eating right, getting physically fit, emotional wellness, spiritual wellness and prevention are all apart of creating a healthy lifestyle. Since the entire Self, meaning all aspects of one's personality, must work in harmony to achieve wellness, you need to put balanced energy into each aspect of yourself. The yoga aims for healthy tuning of all the three bodies (physical, subtle and causal) of a person.

Yogasthah kuru karmaani sangam tyaktvaa dhananjaya /
Siddhyasiddhyoh samo bhuutvaa samatvam yoga ucyate//

Remaining steadfast in *yoga,* oh *Dhananjaya (Arjuna)*, perform actions, abandoning attachment, remaining the same to success and failure alike. This evenness of mind is called yoga.

One of the key themes weaving through the Gita is the relationship between the path of action in the world, *karma-yoga,* and the path of *sannyaasa*, the renunciation of the world to pursue self-knowledge. Karma is any action performed and also the results of those actions, and in these two verses, Krishna presents a two-fold definition of karma-yoga: *samatvam yogah ucyate* and *yogah karmasu kaushalam.*

The body or Physical self requires good nutrition, appropriate weight, beneficial exercise, adequate rest and proper stress management. The mind or emotional self needs self-supportive attitudes, positive thoughts and viewpoints and a positive self-image. You also need to give and receive forgiveness, love and compassion; you need to laugh and experience happiness; you need joyful relationships with yourself and others. The Spiritual self requires inner calmness, openness to your creativity, and trust in your inner knowing. And for some it requires having a relationship with a higher power.

We all know when the Physical self is out of balance, our body tells us right away. We feel fatigue or catch a cold or maybe. But how do we know when the Emotional self or spiritual self are out of balance?

Sit down and outline your definition of healthy living. List all your negative habits, the ones that contribute to your unhealthy lifestyle (i.e. smoking, excessive alcohol consumption). Then take time to list your current health conditions. Taking the 'wellness Quiz' will help identify other significant areas that you need to include while outlining your definition of a Healthy Living. Once you have all your information written down it's time to create your healthy living plan. Below is an outline which can be adapted. You may find this helpful in listing your goals.

Add as many goals as you need to this outline. Once you arrive at a comprehensive idea about the definition of Healthy Living and turn that into a concrete plan, it's time to prioritize. Pick a few of the goals that you feel are most important to your overall health and happiness and start with those. Don't try to do them all at once that's a sure fire way to fail! Start with 2-3 for a month and then add one per month until you have achieved all your goals. Achieving total health requires taking responsibility, making a commitment to you, creating a plan and then taking action. If some one can follow these simple steps he will be on the way to living a healthier life.

VII

Yoga and Education

ROLE OF YOGA IN EDUCATION

Education is a process of growth, development and adding something new to one's experiences. There are two phases involved in the educational process namely teaching and learning. Teaching consists of 'Organization and conduct of learning experience' by the teacher. Learning is an adjustment of the whole organism by the student to a new situation created by the teacher. Teacher is a person who stimulates learning in the student by organizing and guiding certain experiences of the individuals under his leadership. He is essentially an educator who 'brings out' all that is best in the student.

Student is one who desires to adjust his whole organization to a new situation organized and guided by the teacher. Methods are techniques or procedures used by the teacher through which an interaction between teacher and student takes places.

The Scope of Teaching-Learning

The purpose of teaching is to induce change in the student. There can be no teaching unless learning takes place. The teacher merely arranges the environment for learning and stimulates and guides the students' activity in that environment. It is the student who learns and each student has to do his own learning. Teaching serves to bring the student into a learning environment and enhance the efficiency of the learning process.

Teaching is a science in the sense that it involves logical and systematic arrangement based on certain principles. Teaching is also an art, meaning that it cannot be reduced to a formula. Teaching is an art which requires sensitivity to factors affecting the student and his environment for learning and which must be suitably modified according to his needs. The whole educational process involving teaching-learning centers round the most important factor—the student.

At present the only aim of education is to develop the capacity to earn a lot of money and hence Gurukul tradition cannot be introduced; but guardians can at least train them in self-control, altruism, compassion and caring concern for all sentient beings. It is a blunder to marry them off so long as they do not become mature, responsible and self supporting; otherwise they may prove as miserable failures throughout their lives. The condition of a family, whose members neither know the art of living nor have the requisite knowledge and experience of life to opt for it, is as miserable as that of a chariot having un-reined horses. What sorts of conflicts are going on in the families of today running on the pattern of blind beliefs is known to every body.

Education is supposed to have a cleansing, uplifting and refining effect. If this education system is enlivened with inclusion of moral, ethical and spiritual values, it will lead to a new generation of youngsters sizzling with zeal to embrace and uplift the lowliest and the lost by voluntarily educating them in an exclusive pattern, inculcating in them qualities of love, kindness, compassion, sharing and caring. Oure universe can thus become a place worth returning again and again. For social progress and national uplift also every citizen should compulsorily be educated in ethical, moral and spiritual values. Education develops a person's intelligence and makes him fit to earn worldly as well as spiritual boons. There can be no other better way for overall development of life.

Yoga Education

Yoga helps bring about subtle attitudinal changes in life. If taught earlier on in life, they are easily implemented and can bring about a healthy change in society. Being able to harness ambition in a positive manner rather than through negativity will not only help a student excel but also make him a healthier and happier person.

A report published on 15th January 2009 by *Hindustan Times* reflects that: Only 50 per cent of Class V children in Tamil Nadu, Andhra Pradesh and Karnataka can tell time correctly. In business-savvy Gujarat, only 77 per cent students in this class can do currency tasks effectively, behind the national average of 83.2. Only 21 per cent of such children in rural areas can recognize numbers from 10 to 99. Ironically, these are the states with the largest concentration of engineering colleges and they also produce the highest number of techies. But when it comes to basics, they paint a dismal picture.

According to the Annual Status of Education Report, Rural (ASER) 2008, the three southern states, Gujarat and Uttar Pradesh are all lagging way behind the national average (61 per cent) when it comes to children's ability to tell time. These points to the fact telling time and recognizing money is dependent more on the environment in which a child grows up.

This is the situation in rural area; coming to the urban area, here the problem with our children is deferent. According to a research conducted by Vidyasagar Institute of Mental Health and Neuro Science, 74 Lakh children in India are in the grip of Attention Deficit Disorder (ADD). Since, due to ignorance and being busy in work, parents do not happen to pay attention to it, 22 Lakh of these children grow up to become un-social or anti-social.

Dr. Nagpal states in his study that there are three main symptoms of HADD. The first one is lack of concentration, second is hyperactivity and the third is a compulsion to do something. In addition to these symptoms, scattering of mind, unstable and violent behaviour, inferiority complex, doing things that attract people's attention, building castles in the air, tendency of not to stay together, poor memory, lack of patience, behaviour that troubles others, are commonly found in the children affected by this disease. They leave out studies. Often they fail to complete even school education. They get frequent attacks of depression. At such occasions, controlling them becomes very difficult.

The Psychologists concept of moral behaviour is much like the layman's and psychoanalysts concept of conscience or moral character (Donselson 1973). Morality is inferred from a person's intrinsically motivated resistance to temptation and from his guilt feeling that follow acts of transgression. Moral values play an important role in shaping personality development of children.

Professor Hans Kraus, former physician to J.F. Kennedy insists that our inactive and overindulgent way of life is particularly dangerous for children who should be building up strong muscles for their adult years. Prof. Kraus point out that some form of physical activities like yoga is essential for all children.

Yoga Eduction and Moral Values

Indian sages had stressed that character can be made strong and noble in childhood only. Advancement in age makes the character traits very rigid. Only those who went through a regimen of self-control and self refinement in childhood can become great, intelligent and spiritually elevated. So long as this tradition continued properly there was no lack of happiness, peace and prosperity in society—which is a collection of individuals.

This important aspect of character building in children is neglected today, which is a matter of deep concern. Seeing the speed with which moral crimes are increasing in children, social reformers are bound to be worried. When hatred and vices get deeply rooted in nature at young age no reformative programmes would give desired success even with great efforts. Practical difficulty is that the guardians do not bear this responsibility consciously and seriously. Most of them do not even know how to inculcate nobility of character in children. Self-willed children adopt only evils and vices of society because they are surrounded by them only. Formation of personality starts in the womb itself. Keeping in mind this fact Indian rishis introduced ritual system (sanskars). This gave the children moral training in a natural manner.

Yoga should be properly introduced to children by educators. In the opinion of Swami Satyananda Saraswati, all the experiments that are being done in every part of the world in relation to the educational system should be compiled. A lot has been said and a lot is being done. Science is very clear about the effect of Yoga on the brain and on human consciousness and character. The time has come to decide how to implement this as a practical scheme.

Moral values are the standards of good and evil, which govern an individual's behaviour and choices. Individual's morals may derive be from society and government, religion, or self. When moral values derive from society and government they, of necessity, may change as the laws and morals of the society change. Children are not just little adults. They go through typical characteristics of growth—intellectually, emotionally, and socially—on their way to becoming adults. When parents realize these things, there is less strain on both parents and children. Remembering that a child does not think like an adult, have the same attention span, or see the world the same way adults do, can help a parent plan a home which everyone can enjoy.

These days parents or guardians do not or cannot pay as much attention to children as is necessary. Prof. Jean Huston in his book "Child Care: Its Psychological Meaning", has presented the research experiments done on the activities of children and the conclusion there of. He says that in one case parents get so busy in their jobs those children are left to be taken care of by servants and material provisions. They do not have enough time to spare for their children. In an other case the parents pay over attention to the children. All their just and unjust demands are fulfilled or they are kept under too much strict watch, which hinders their independent development.

Prof. Huston says that in bringing up children, we should have the skill of a gardener. There should not be so much lack of care as not to provide for the needs necessary for growth nor there so much excessive caring as to deprive them from availing natural nourishment. In order that children obey you and become less mischievous, it is necessary for the parents to bring about an attitudinal change in them in certain respects.

For cultural elevation, we should develop our life by introspection and purification but should not forget that with this much only it will not be possible to raise our culture to a per-eminent place in the world. The greatest need of today is the personality development of our children. The day our children get morally and ethically elevated the time will not be far when dignity of our society will again start attracting world attention.

ROLE OF YOGA TOWARDS PERSONALITY DEVELOPMENT

Personality is a set of qualities that make a person (or thing) distinct from another; An assumed role or manner of behaviour; qualities that make a person stand out from the crowd—the complexities of all the attributes—behavioural, temperamental, emotional and mental—characterize a unique individual.

Concept of Personality

Personality can be defined as a dynamic and organized set of characteristics possessed by a person with uniquely influences his or her cognitions, motivations, and behaviours in various situations. The word "personality" originates from the Latin *persona*, which means mask. Significantly, in the theatre of the ancient Latin-speaking world, the mask was not used as a plot device to *disguise* the identity of a character, but rather was a convention employed to represent or *typify* that character.

Personality can be divided into three types: Type A, Type B and Type AB. Type A individuals can be described as impatient, time-conscious, controlling, concerned about their status, highly competitive, ambitious, business—like, aggressive, having difficulty relaxing; and are sometimes disliked by individuals with Type B personalities for the way that they're always rushing. They are often high-achieving workaholics who multi-task, drive themselves with deadlines, and are unhappy about delays. Because of these characteristics, Type A individuals are often described as "stress junkies."

Type B individuals, in contrast, are described as patient, relaxed, and easy-going, generally lacking an overriding sense of urgency. This can also be described as lazy and lacking ambition. People who live in their mother's basements are an example. Because of these characteristics, Type B individuals are often described by Type A's as apathetic and disengaged. There is also a Type AB mixed profile for people who cannot be clearly categorized.

Development of Personality

Personality Development quintessentially means enhancing and grooming one's outer and inner self to bring about a positive change to ones life. Personality development is an art to have a magnetic personality, which everyone want to achieve.

> *Priyam ma krnu devesu priyam rajasu ma krnu*
> *Priyam sarvasya pasyata uta sudra utarye.*
>
> —Atharvaveda 19/62/1

Meaning: O Lord! Make me dear to gods. Make me dear to kings.

May I be dear to all the viewers, be they sudra or vaisya (the servitors or the professionals).

Attractive personality is acquired by the judicious mixture of strength and emotions. The better the synthesis of these two elements, the more magnetic and charming the personality will be. Both the attributes are doubtlessly essential but their real significance and meaning lies in their proper synthesis. In isolation, either of the two loses its effectiveness. Strength alone without emotion and sensitivity does make a person capable and competent, but simultaneously makes him cruel hearted too. Consequently, people, even as they feel attracted to powerful person, also remain inwardly scared of him.

The same is the case with emotions without strength. In this condition, the personality develops tender feelings but lacks in determination and competence. This type acquires "the poor fellow" image inviting from the people a patronizing attitude. Such a personality can be anything but attractive.

It is true that the thinking and behaviour of such a person touch the inner chords of those who come in contact, but for want of sufficient capability he is unable to provide them any succor. All the tender emotions in life can not add up to power and strength, and such persons are generally forced to lead the life of an imaginative and emotional but weak person.

Therefore, if you are desirous of making yourself magnetic, combine your strengths with emotions and then see how soon you become the centre of everybody's attraction. People of every age, class and qualification will vie with one another to be near you. The world will hold you up as a role model; it will talk about you, dream about you and want to become like you. Whether you are a man or woman, farmer or officer, student or housewife, it does not matter. In every condition and every situation, the doors to personality furbishing are open to you. You have only to make a start.

The first step is to get ready to make the body and mind receptive and deserving. Remember, body becomes capable by self-control and mind by introspection and contemplation. A disciplined and regulated lifestyle and light physical exercises impart a certain beauteous luster to the body.

For proper expression of this beauty, the dress should be in tune with the place and occasion. In this connection, the important thing to always bear in mind is that the real source of the accentuated charm of the body is the subtle vital energy and this vitality comes only by tapa and continence. Purity and piety increase person's vital force whereas unrestrained sensual proclivities sap it. To maintain attractiveness for a long time, one has to retain vitality and vigor for long too.

To become capable and strong mentaly, develop the habit of introspection because it helps promote one's abilities and hidden talents. Identify what is your special talent, your innate aptitude and set about to work on that. It could by anything music, sports, management, house-keeping, or any other branch of knowledge and art. If you find yourself unable to identify it, consult your friends, or guardians. Do not lag behind at any level in the you striving for talent nurturing.

Physical strength and mental prowess make one powerful. Now the turn is of the virtuous qualities that give expression to this power. So, try your utmost to inculcate the qualities of courage, bravery, patience and fortitude in you. Make yoga practice a part of your life. As purification and asana strengthen your body, practice of pranayama makes the individual pranically and mentally strong. Practice of meditation makes you emotionally mature and spiritually evolved.

These attributes will make you the sinecure of all eyes, not only at home and in the immediate locality but the society at large. Only the virtuous and the righteous radiate real magnetic, not the vicious and the wicked. Even the latter need a cloak of virtues to look attractive. It is another matter that after the spurious façade is gone, they are in for great ridicule and derision. The truly virtuous, on the other hand, retain their pull till the last breath.

Besides being strong and capable, one must be sensitive and emotional, because power without sensitivity makes a person arrogant. People will soon start running away from him. The three expressions of sensitivity presently relevant here are; (i) service to the needy, (ii) generosity, and (iii) tolerance. You will be able to develop your abilities through the instrumentality of all the three.

In this way, the Yoga sadhana of combining strength and emotion will continue to add charm to your personality. But you will have to remain continually vigilant for its full and effective expression.

VIII

Methods of Teaching Yoga

TEACHING METHODOLOGY IN YOGA

Having knowledge of Yoga is helpful in individual practice but teaching Yoga is totally different. Beyond the knowledge of Yoga in the area of basic philosophy, the different paths of Yoga, the practice of meditation, asana, and Pranayama etc, there is still much more for an expert to learn about teaching Yoga. These subjects need some attention, for an aspirant of Yoga. When an intern has successfully graduated, Yoga becomes a part of daily independent research or continuing education.

Teaching Yoga is something like sharing one's own experience of practicing Yoga to the others. Teaching methodology of Yoga can be implemented through instructing classes. Interns should have a firm grasp of the principles, practices, and procedures involved in teaching classes. Upon successful graduation, interns can learn the necessary procedures and techniques involved in teaching Yoga.

Principles of Yoga Teaching

The first principle of Yoga teaching is: the Instructor should be a regular practitioner. Maharshi Patanjali states: *Sa tu dīrgha-kāla-nairantarya-satkārāsevito dṛdha-bhūmiḥ* i.e. regular and constant practice of a holy work gives a firm ground to the aspirant. The personal practice of interns and Yoga teachers should be a part of daily life. To read Yogic philosophy, meditate, practice pranayama, and practice asana should be a structured part of each day. This also allows time for exploring your own practice and developing solutions for your students.

Some of the points have been radiated here, which the teacher should keep in the mind, for Teaching Yoga. Firstly one should be aware whether he is going to teach Yoga to a group or an individual.

The second thing is which group is in front of you; whether they are children, young, old age people or the sick persons. A competent Yoga instructor should be able to teach anyone, regardless of their physical ability. We can adapt our teaching style to suit the physical abilities or limitations of our students. A Yoga class should not be a "trial by fire" for new students. Hence, the graduate of a well-rounded teacher training course should be able to teach a wide variety of students in different stages of health.

The next point is which tools you are going to be used? Whether it is a classroom? A lecture cum Demonstration Method of Presentation in Yoga teaching is the best. Some Yoga instructors feel that his method for teaching Yoga is better than the rest; but which one is it? If a Yoga teacher does not give a physical assist, is that wrong? If a Yoga instructor does not demonstrate poses, how can students who learn visually make progress?

The Yoga instructor who helps before verbally cueing may not be harmful but again individually correcting the poses will take lot of time and rest of the participants may not be taking interest in such conditions. Sometimes, some students just do not feel comfortable getting physical assistance from their Yoga teacher. So, what do you do? Firstly, before giving assistance, during Asana practice, a Yoga teacher should take permission. If anyone has an objection, you are better off to demonstrate the Yoga technique or explain it verbally. It is not worth the potential conflict, and each Yoga student has a right to his, or her, own space. It is said that one has to "Tread carefully" when volunteering to give a physical assistance to any Yoga student.

Role of Language, Voice, Fluency, Clarity and Body Language are the next points to be understood in Teaching Yoga. There are many methods for teaching Yoga, but students either learn by seeing, feeling, hearing, or a combination of senses. With this in mind, there is no right or wrong method, but Yoga teachers should be aware that some students may have a dominant sense when it comes to learning. This is why teaching methods for Yoga should be integrated. There will always be a Yoga student who does not like your method, but you should be able to effectively communicate with the vast majority of your students.

Always be aware that what you are going to teach should be Conceptual and Practical. There are times when, despite all the verbal cueing of skills imaginable, a Yoga teacher must make a physical assistance. No matter what is said, some Yoga students will learn more from a solid assistance than by cueing. This helps a student "feel" where he or she should be. A verbal explanation is close, but is not the same as feeling proper alignment while an Asana is practiced.

Another point is Presentation of Lessons in Specific Yogic Practices. The teacher should have the preparation before starting the class. Demonstrating Asanas also has its pitfalls for Yoga teachers. Too much demonstrating can make some Yoga students feel like they are just an extension of your workout. Too little demonstrating and some Yoga students may grumble that it is easy for the Yoga teacher to say, when the Yoga teacher is "just walking around." So, what do you do to please your Yoga students?

The next point is preparing a Lesson Plan. Make sure your Yoga students are exposed to a combination of Assisting, Demonstrating, and Verbal Cues. In this way, you will have satisfied most of them. There is a "stepping stone" process for learning how to teach Yoga. The first step is careful observation of other teachers. Learn what you would, and would not, do by participating in a class. This form of observation requires the intern to participate, and take in the whole classroom experience, in complete silence.

Class Management while Conducting Yoga classes is an art. Learning to adjust, modify, and assist for alignment is the second step. Work with everyone who will allow you to. This will require some repetitive homework. Repetition is the best way to become comfortable with assisting.

Critical observation of a Yoga class is another important issue. In Yoga teaching there is a need for individual attention and Customized teaching methods for every student. Some interns act as assistants to a Yoga teacher during a class. The assistants will help students with modifications, props, alignment, and physical assists. This is a great way to gain experience. Once this has been mastered, teaching friends in small groups, semi-private, or private sessions is a good way to develop inner confidence. This is difficult, if you are from a culture where men and women do not casually touch each other.

One thing should be very clear—what are the purpose and needs of practising, teaching or organizing Yoga class? If you concentrate on each step of development, you will be successful. No step should be by-passed. Some Yoga teachers never develop a sense for modifications, using props, proper alignment, or giving an assist. You never want to be one of them.

Precautions and Contraindications of practices is one of the important issues in Yoga Teaching. It is inevitable that you will find students who have poor health conditions. This will require you to become an innovator. To imitate your best teachers is a wonderful compliment to them, but to eventually become creative is a testament to the entire Yoga teacher training process.

Organizing Yoga Classes or Yoga camps should be the hobby of the Yoga teacher. If you are not enjoying your class, just try to find out the loop holes. Either this job is not for you, or join a workshop to improve your teaching. The best teacher is one who tries to learn from every situation. Use of different Techniques which may be new for you is not wrong to apply. There are several organizations for Attitude Training; they may help to improve Yoga Teaching.

Methods of Teaching

During the process of teaching several methods have been tried over many years and we find that they fall into two main categories:

(i) Instructional methods used in the classroom for teaching theoretical subjects.
(ii) Methods used for teaching practical skill on the fields or in gymnasiums.

The classroom methods are variously named the lecture method, the recitation method, the project method, the laboratory method, the dramatic method and the group discussion method. The methods for teaching skills or physical activities, however, have not been properly categorized. Each method used in the classroom situation has many implications for teaching physical activities and skills, but they cannot be directly applied to teaching physical activities and skills. Even in respect of classroom teaching, no single method or pattern could serve as the best method for all teaching situations. The method of teaching yogic practices comes closer to that of physical activities rather than theoretical subjects.

Traditionally, there have been two approaches towards successful teaching: the first is a teacher-centered approach and the second a student-centered approach.

The teacher-centered approach was the main method in the past, even in Yoga. But today scientific thought focuses its attention on and emphasizes the student-centered approach.

So naturally, the principles and concepts which underlie the methods are expected to involve this student-centered approach, the main emphasis of which is due consideration of the needs of the students. Methods of teaching must be compatible with the goals sought or the outcomes expected.

The purpose of any method is to create learning in the student. The teacher should know how a particular method he uses affects the student's learning ability. The following are some of the basic methods of teaching:

Lecture Method

It is perhaps the oldest method used for formal teaching. It is valuable in organizing large fields on material, separating a particular type of information for immediate use, presenting new information and synthesizing information from a wide variety of sources.

It is more useful with mature students having a high degree of auditory perception since it involves attention, voice level, clarity, use of rest period and vocabulary level.

The lecture has considerable use in teaching yogic practices. It may be used in presenting any type of information related to particular activity in the perspective of yoga in general.

When extensive lecture is necessary for the achievement of a specific goal, the students should be able to hear the teacher clearly. A lecture can be stimulating interesting and motivating to the students if the teacher prepares it properly. The lecture method proves of greater advantage when combined with other methods. The use of visual materials is of considerable help in aiding students to retain the content of the lecture.

When using the lecture method the teacher should also be aware of the limitations of this method, which may be mentioned as follows:

(i) It is a teacher-centered activity and may encourage lack of participation on the part of the students.
(ii) Many student lack ability to earn by this method.
(iii) It may lead teachers to ignore more effective methods.
(iv) The attention span of more immature students is too short to benefit from a long lecture.

Response-to-Instruction Method

In this method the teacher gives precise instructions which precede, follow or are concurrent with a demonstration and all students respond to the instructions of the teacher in the same way.

There is very little attention paid to the individuals. The emphasis is on the subject matter of activity that is introduced. This method has a formal approach. An information approach with this method is more favourable in teaching such activities where there is some variation in the performance of individuals. This method can be profitably used after due attention to problems of individuals.

Individualized Instructional Method

It is based on the principle that learning is highly individualized. In this method attempts are made to provide by different means for individual differences within the pattern of the group structure.

Directed-Practice Method

Assignments for extra practice of selected yogic practices out of class hours enhance skill and performance levels of the students. Necessary introduction along with the preliminary practice of selected yogic exercises like Sirasasana, Uddiyana, Kapalabhati, Nauli,

Purificatory processes etc. may be done in the class and the efficiency could be developed through out-of-class practice. The students should be encouraged to do out-of-class practices and the teacher may check the results during subsequent classes and give additional suggestions for further practice. Obviously, the success of this method depends upon motivation of the students and their rapport with the teacher.

Project Method

The aim of this method is to enable the students to put into practice what they have learned in the class. It may also be of help for students to learn related information. When the time is short in the regular schedule, projects such as preparing notes on the yogic practices undergone, collection of related material from various sources, preparing models and the exhibits of the yogic practices, planned observations of seminars, conferences, competitions related to yogic activities as well as visits to different wellknown yoga centers are of great value.

Demonstration Method

Demonstration refers to non-competitive type performances with emphasis on skill and form. Demonstrations are of value, if properly directed to both performer and viewer. The Demonstration method describes the organization of the teaching of the class with the sole purpose of public demonstration when concluded. Demonstration method as a technique for the use of the class has some disadvantages. The scope of learning is restricted. It utilizes existing talent rather than developing new skills. However, the demonstration method serves as an excellent group method.

Unfortunately, there appears to be no simple formula for selecting the best methods. This depends on the conditions available, such as time, space and equipment. The teacher should have the skill to use a particular method and adapt it to prevailing conditions so that the students receive proper orientation and understanding of the technique and purpose of the method. In other words, a method should always be considered as a means to an end and not the end in itself. It should allow for individual differences and in itself. The method should allow for individual differences and stimulate both creativity and independent thinking in the students. In Yoga, the teaching method has to be eclectic, drawing upon useful vital contributions from several exiting methods.

Factors Influencing the Method

The following factors govern the selection of particular method or combination of methods: It has beem already seen that the method of teaching depends upon the nature of the subject and that the practical subject requires a different method from the theoretical subject.

Even different practical skills require different methods. We know also that the method of teaching skills in Physical Education comes closer to the teaching of yogic practices due to the similarity of content.

The method of teaching differs according to the previous experience of the students. Progressive skills cannot be taught to those who have not already mastered the basic skills. The teacher can save time and energy by enquiring about students' previous experience in the skill to be learned.

The Teacher

Efficiency of method depends on the teacher who uses it. Method itself is neither good nor bad. It turns out to be good in the hands of an able teacher. The teacher does influence the method selected. They have the following qualities which are all reflected through the chosen method:

(i) A genuine interest in communication.
(ii) Love of the work of teaching.
(iii) A willingness to share interest and experiences with others.
(iv) An ability to put him or herself in the position of the student.
(v) The capacity for understanding expressed in an open, authentic way without blaming or condemning the students.
(vi) An attractive personality.
(vii) The ability to set a good example through lifestyle and behaviour.
(viii) A sense of professional responsibility towards the students.
(ix) A pleasant, yet commanding voice.
(x) The awareness that, "The person in the teacher is more important that the method".

Suitable modifications in the method depending upon the needs of the students and time framework are possible only when the teacher is conscious of the situation he is handling.

The art of teaching on the part of the teacher depends on the suitable modifications in the teaching method routinely used.

Facilities

Availability of facilities greatly influences the teaching method. It becomes more efficient with the necessary facilities. In the absence of required facilities the teacher sometimes feels insecure, tense and is unable to give of his or her best. These facilities could be in the form of an adequate space, necessary equipment and congenial atmosphere. For example, if there is no hall for teaching Asanas and the class is required to be conducted on an open ground, the teacher will face the problem while doing Asanas in the lying position. If there are no water facilities available, purificatory processes or kriyas will have limitations for teaching. If the atmosphere is noisy, teaching or demonstrating meditation techniques will be difficult.

An effective teaching method depends on the knowledge of important principles of anatomy, physiology, psychology, pedagogy and yoga so that the teacher may be flexible in modifying the method. These principles also provide sound base for selection and formulation of methods.

Sources of Teaching Method

The teacher should be well acquainted with the variety of important principles drawn from education, yogic discipline, psychology of learning, anatomy and physiology in order to formulate good teaching methods.

Basic Principles of Yoga

(i) Yogic practices are not 'exercises' as we understand them. The word is generally applied to vigorous physical movements. Since Yogic practices do not involve vigorous movements any kind of violent action should be avoided during yoga practice.
(ii) The nature of yogic practices is varied and involves different mechanisms through which the results of particular yogic practices are obtained. The Asana, Pranayama, Bandhas, Mudras, kriyas and Meditation do not use the same channels for bringing the result of the practices.
(iii) Asana—one of the most important and best known of the yogic practices—are 'static stretching procedures'. They should be performed slowly and smoothly in order to influence the tonic system rather than the phasic one.
(iv) The position in a particular asana should be comfortably maintained for some time with least effort. Effortless performance and relaxing as much as possible during the final position are the chief characteristics of the technique of Asanas.
(v) Pranayamic practices are very different in purpose and technique from the 'Breathing exercises'. They are supposed to increase oxygen intake. However, they are considered of little value in the literature of Physical Education.
(vi) Yogic practices should not lead to undue fatigue. If there is fatigue it should be overcome by the practice of relaxation in Shavasana.
(vii) All yogic practices should be performed according to one's own capacity and without competition with others.
(viii) All yogic practices should lead to peace of mind.
(ix) Any yogic routine should begin with psycho-physical relaxation, centering one's attention as one would in prayer, or actual recitation of some prayers.

Psychological Principles

(i) Interest is the best motivation for learning. The teacher should teach in such a way that students maintain their interest and motivation to learn.

(ii) Activity is necessary for learning. Learning is a process of experience. Unless the student is involves in the experience of activity he/she may not be able to learn. Therefore practice is essential, especially for motorlearning or skill-learning. Again it is not mere practice but it the correct practice that is important. Complex motor skills require more repetitions of correct practice.

(iii) All learning has a neural basis. Unless proper neuromuscular coordination is formed one cannot expect further developments in any motor skills.

(iv) For efficient learning the material to be learnt must be within the range of experience and abilities of the learner. Learning is highly individualized and results in progressive changes in behaviour. The ability to learn depends upon the innate capacity and previous experiences of the student. All individuals do not learn at the same rate.

(v) Learning of motor skills is hastened if the performer is able to grasp an intellectual understanding of the nature of the task before beginning the practice.

(vi) Regular practice of an activity resulting in pleasure and satisfaction contributes to the most effective learning.

(vii) Occasional short periods of rest between the practice periods produce superior results in learning motor skills. Brief rest period prevent fatigue in the muscles and efficiency of the muscles is not decreased.

Physiological Principles

1. Age and Sex are the two important factors determining the anatomicophysiological conditions which need to be considered in the teaching learning process of motor activities. There are anatomical differences between the male and the female. One of the main differences to be taken into account is the structure. Generally, women are considered to be weaker in structure than men. This means that both bones and ankles are not as strong and their bodies have more fatty tissue. The male body is composed of 41.8 per cent of the body weight of muscle, while the female body has 35.8 per cent. The distribution of fatty tissue is 18.2 per cent of the body weight in males and 28.2 per cent in females. Hence this gives men more muscular strength than women.
2. The muscle strength is proportionate to the amount of fat to muscle tissue. The more fat there is obviously the less efficient are the muscles. Reduction in fat therefore, contributes to building of muscle strength.
3. The abdominal wall can also be weaker in women from a mechanical

point of view. Women's abdominal organs are not firmly situated and the abdominal tone is often lost through childbirth, miscarriages or other reproductive problems.

4. There are differences also in the proportions of the different segments of the spinal column. Specially in the lumbar region which affects performance of physical movements. The shorter lumbar and thoracic regions in the female sometimes produce a more pronounced shortening of lower back muscles resulting in lordosis. The lumbo-sacral angle is also different: 138 in female and 133 in male.
5. The tone of the muscles influences to a considerable extent the posture and functions of the body organs of an individual. Muscle tone is a sort of sustained contraction of the muscle fibres. Cultivation of improved muscle tone implies relaxation of undue tensions as well as increase of tone of habitually slack muscles. It is accompanied by an increased awareness of the entire body. One becomes aware of undue tensions in the body and learns to relax more and more when one is attempting to regain proper tone. Improvement of muscle tone brings corresponding improvement in equilibrium, circulation and neuroglandular activity. Static stretching of the muscles contributes to the proper development of muscle tone.
6. Abdominal muscles play an important role in holding the abdominal viscera in place. The tone of the abdominal muscles governs the efficient functioning of the organs situated in the abdominal cavity.
7. Muscle efficiency is lost during long periods of inactivity, especially, if the activity is caused by illness. Under such circumstances any physical activity demanding exertion should be introduced slowly and cautiously.
8. Fatigue is not confined exclusively to the particular muscles exercised. But it spreads through the body as a whole to some degree. Hence to remove fatigue, relaxation of the whole body is desirable.
9. The equilibrium of the body involves muscular co-ordination and proper functioning of the semicircular canals of the internal ears, the eyes, the receptors in the skin and nerve endings in muscles and ligaments around joints.
10. Minimum expenditure of energy is the criterion of simplicity and efficiency in any activity. Vigorous movements consume more energy, while static activities consume less energy.
11. The theory and practice of warming up needs consideration when one engages in vigorous, dynamic and jerky activities. It is not relevant in static activity.
12. The centre of gravity in female bodies is lower than in males. This should be taken into consideration in practices involving stability and balance.

Educational Principles

1. Learning depends upon impressions received by the necessary receptors.
   Five senses represent the avenues of learning. Therefore the presentation of a specific practice or skill should involve as many senses as possible to form an adequate image of the practice.

   However, the most important cues in practice come from audio-visual aids. Motor learning is perceptual, cognitive, rational, thoughtful and involves mental as well as physical aspects of learning. The ideas must be translated into muscular action.

   There are individual differences in effectively utilizing various kinds of sensory information. Some individuals have remarkable ability to organize visually presented information quickly. Others synthesise information and analyse the situation, hence appear to respond more slowly.

   Visual demonstration of the practice is one of the most effective way to enhance the learning of a motor skill. However, learning is hastened if the student is able to have an intellectual understanding of the nature of the task before the beginning of the practice and is given sometime to integrate the initial cues from observing the demonstration and listening to instructions. Brief, clear descriptions of the activity with repeated demonstrations and pointing out likely faults bring good results.
2. At the preliminary stages, 'Over learning' through repeated practice is necessary. The emphasis should be on aiming at right or correct practice. This can be done by specific instructions. Instructions may also be divided into those offered before the performance of the activity, those which accompany performance and those by way of information or corrections at the end of the performance of the activity.

   Formal instructions are best suited during the initial phases of the learning process. Initial instructions prevent the student from adopting incorrect habits that might later have to be unlearned.

   Students should be instructed in the positive way of performing the activity rather than being informed initially what to avoid. However, best performance comes when individuals are informed both what to do and what to avoid.

   This helps in learning the activity by eliminating possible errors as well as increasing such positive aspects as ease, comfort, efficiency, lowering of tension during performance and speed in some respects.
3. Adequate time should be allotted for actual practice without which learning cannot be effective. The practice period should be divided into informal practice and supervised practice in a group.

4. The 'Principle of Progression' is vital to learning. It means performance of any activity from "simple to complex" and from "known to unknown".

   This principle rests upon a sound neuro-muscular basis. Complex motor learning requires an order of pre-requisites, a background of specific attainments. The learning of co-ordinated movement patterns is dependent upon the possession of sufficient amount of fundamental physical abilities such as muscular strength, flexibility, muscular endurance and cardiorespiratory endurance. This obvious relationship is sometimes ignored, but effective learning is possible only when this relationship is kept in mind.

   The whole programme of activities should therefore be planned and conducted in the light of the principle of progression.

5. Effective learning takes place through the use of the Whole Method, Part Method or a combination of Whole and Part Methods. The combination method id also called Progressive Part Method or Repetitive Part or Continuous Part Method. The use of any of these methods depends on the degree of complexity of the activity.

   (a) The Whole Method consists in presenting the activity in its entirety without any division. If the activity to be learnt is not complex and the learner is mature, the whole method is suitable.

   (b) The Part Method is based on analysis of the purpose and of identifying a logical sequence of parts for presentation from simple to complex.

   The part method is better if the student is immature and/or the activity complex.

   (c) Progressive Part Method is more often used than the part method. In this method a part is learned, paired with the second part and the two practiced together. Then the third part is practiced and three parts practiced as a whole until the entire activity is constructed.

   Methods of presentation may stress formal instructions or informal suggestions. But the fundamental basis of all methods is the nature and need of the students, including their individual and group characteristics in learning. The nature of educational objectives and the type of activities used in the programme also dictate the choice of methods.

6. The teacher's interest and attitude towards the students determine to great extent adequate learning. There is a need on the part of the teacher to inspire the student to accurate and satisfactory performance. If the student is not performing correctly he should be shown the points where he/she makes mistakes in a positive way that encourages self-correction.

7. Learning does not take place unless there is some way for the performer to assess his/her relative success or failure. Although it is necessary to correct faulty performance, too many corrections at a time can be confusing. The teacher should correct the most important fault first. Most corrections should be in the form of positive suggestions.
8. Immediately after the ideal demonstration of the activity the opportunity to try out and practice the activity should be provided for the students.
9. The teacher should encourage students to ask any questions related to the activity, listen to what each person has to say and try to understand his problem. Never discourage or ridicule even a trifling question. It may add to new thinking on the part of the teacher. Give a suitable answer to his satisfaction and/or use the question to open a discussion in the class as a whole if necessary.

Sociological Principles

Utility Value

The idea of utility need not necessarily be interpreted in the light of activities involved in earning a living alone. Many activities and experiences are of real practical use in helping the person to live happily and successfully that are not of any immediate vocational significance. Yogic practices may not necessarily be of vocational value but they are certainly of immediate practical use for a person of any age and sex in maintaining good health and physical fitness together

Class Management

Students rarely cause trouble when they are interested and when suitable lesson content is presented in a competent and stimulating fashion. One essential thing in reducing the problem of control to a minimum is to create an atmosphere of natural freedom, friendliness, mutual help and understanding. These qualities in a class should emanate from the leadership of the teacher. This develops social consciousness in students and an awareness of their responsibility to the group.

The students or participants of Yoga may be grouped under the following headings:

- Beginners
- Experienced and advanced
- School children
- Special attention Groups

(a) *Beginners.* This group may involve persons of all ages, males and females, young and old and special individuals who are making their first acquaintance with yoga. They need a general background of yogic discipline and motivation to continue with yoga.

(b) *Experienced or Advanced.* This group may consist of persons who have some experience with yoga and wish to advance further to gain more vaired and deeper experience. Their expectation is to acquaint themselves with a greater number of yogic practices and indulge in subtler and higher practices intensively.

(c) *School Children.* This is a select group ranging from the age of 6 years to 18 years and commands largest percentage of the society. School children need exposure to the field of yoga based on the immediate needs of their age and temperament.

(d) *Special Attention Groups.* These individuals can vary on the basis of age like children and adults; on the basis of sex like males and females: on the basis of age and sex like boys and girls; on the basis of individual problems of health, abnormality or handicaps. All these individuals need special attention which is possible in a homogeneous group but not in a heterogeneous group.

Dealing with Difficult Students

The following techniques are useful in dealing with inattentive, talkative or difficult students.

1. Individual students who are disturbing the class may have their attention directed by pausing during instruction, glancing in the direction of the particular student, calling his or her name and asking a question, or if the disturbance is troubling the rest of the class, it should also be pointed out that he is preventing others who are paying attention and working well from hearing the instructions. Alternately, the class can be switched over to another activity.
2. It may help to separate people who talk perpetually but if these students continue to cause disturbance after a few warnings, they should be sent out of the class for a short period. However, it is important to bring the person back soon in the class and to let him or her know that improved behaviour is expected.

In addition, the teacher will have more control if he or she avoids being too familiar with older students. Be friendly but maintain your dignity and social distance. Remember that you are their teacher. Also never allow yourself to become antagonistic towards a student. Your effectiveness in helping him will depend upon your patience and understanding.

Seating Arrangement

The organisation of the class may have any suitable form of seating either in lines, rows, a semi-circle or small circle. Consider that each student needs about 40 square feet and arrange your room accordingly. It is preferable if the floor is covered with a carpet but if this is not possible the floor should be clean and each student should use his own mat. In either case it is desirable that the mat or carpet is covered by a clean sheet of cloth of 6 feet x 3 feet.

The seat of the teacher should be such that the teacher is visible to every student. If the group is large a platform is necessary for the teacher to be visible. In a small group a semi-circle is more suitable as it allows every student to see the teacher clearly. When a platform is used, a revolving one is ideal.

The hall or room where the class is conducted should be well ventilated. It should be well lit so that not only is the class able to see the teacher but the teacher should have a clear view of the class when he is teaching from the platform and while moving about for teaching and answering questions. The practice room or hall should be as quiet as possible and free from any disturbance.

Instructions

Learning of a particular yoga practice depends upon precise instructions by the teacher.

Formal instructions are best suited during the initial stage of learning the practice. Instructions could be divided into those that are given verbally before the beginning of the yogic practice, those which accompany performance of the activity individually or by the group and those that are extended by way of information or corrections after the completion of the activity. Initial instructions prevent the student from adopting incorrect habits which might have to be unlearned later. Practical instructions guide the students for correct and efficient performance.

The following guidelines can help the teacher convey instructions clearly:

(i) Be sure that you have the attention of everyone in the class before any instructions are given.

(ii) When a long explanation is needed it is best to have the class sit down and if necessary closer to the teacher.

(iii) Make your instructions brief, perfectly clear and spoken slowly and distinctly.

(iv) The instructions should be given for only one thing at a time.

(v) Try to use different words and expressions to catch the attention of the students. For example, if students do not understand the first time, use different words in repeating the instructions.

(vi) Describe the technique and procedure of any activity before the students are actually asked to practice.

Audio-Visual Aids

The progress of science in various fields has developed techniques that have made knowledge widely available. These radically alter our systems of communication. The use of computers, for example, has reduced the need for man-power in the area of teaching.

Several groups of students in different locations can be served from a single source which can show the same programme to many different groups. There are many revolutionary possibilities opening up the field of communication through such media as television, video, satellite etc. This is a new phase in our history and these media have immense possibilities for teaching an enormous number of people.

Although sophisticated audio-visual aids are not always within the reach of the teacher, it is necessary to realize the importance of these aids in the learning, process. A teaching aid provides quick information about the subject matter to the students. It gives the teacher a better opportunity of conveying the meaning of what he is saying. It helps the students at all levels to grasp the important points in a class situation. It helps to make the lesson interesting and students are more receptive. Hence it is a very important aspect of teaching method. The response of the students is the best way to judge whether the aid is effective or not, but even if the teacher cannot tell this in advance he should, nevertheless, know the basic principles of preparing and using the aids.

The various teaching aids which are mostly used include backboards, bulletin boards, pictures of all kinds diagrams, sketches, drawings, charts, models, projected devices such as filmstrips, slides, motion pictures and recordings, video-cassettes and television. Visual demonstration is one of the most effective aids to enhance the learning of a motor activity. There is individual difference related to the manner in which various kinds of sensory information are effectively used by the students. Some students have remarkable ability to quickly organize visually presented information. It is desirable that the teacher himself gives the demonstration of a particular yoga practice. The teacher can communicate with his students better through the demonstration staged by him. At the same time he should verbally explain clearly the fundamental principles underlying the yoga practice. Any practice by the students must be preceded by visual demonstration to be effective.

Discussion

A small question-answer session is very helpful at the end of the lesson to evaluate the outcome and remove any difficulties on the part of the students.

The following hints will be useful in conducting a question-answer or discussion session.

(i) Encourage the students to ask their questions or address their comments to the group for discussion.
(ii) Never discourage or ridicule any student's question or contribution whatever small it may be.
(iii) Try to draw all students into discussion rather than a few who are always ready to talk.
(iv) It is wise to limit the discussion to a few important points.
(v) The teacher is expected to know more than the students on the points of discussion. If the teacher is not prepared to answer any question or doses not know any point he should not hesitate to say so, and should say that he will find out the answer and explain that at the next meeting.
(vi) Remember that young children are not mature enough to participate in a group discussion so a different approach is necessary in encouraging them to share their experience.
(vii) Exercise some control over the time spent on questions. Steer the discussion to important and relevant questions. Do not sacrifice valuable time on those points that are not important.

Extra-Class Practice

Once the yoga practice is introduced and techniques explained to the students, it is desirable that they are encouraged to practice on their own at home. All kinds of motivation for the practice at home should be given and they should be assured of all help for correction, modification, improvement from the teacher when they meet next.

Lesson Plan

Preparing a Model Lesson Plan helps the Yoga Teacher. After completing of few sessions the instructor should also have the observation of the outcome of the class, whether this way of teaching the participants are fruitful or not. Apart from that it should also be understood whether the students are taking interest in this method or not. Later on the teacher should prepare a Model lesson plan for that individual or the group.

We have seen earlier that the purpose of teaching is to cause desirable change in the student. Successful planning is necessary on the part of a teacher in order to fulfil this purpose. A plan of each lesson should therefore be prepared.

The advantages of a written lesson plan are:

(i) It helps the teacher to organize his thinking.
(ii) It increases the teacher's confidence and prevents him or her form losing direction during the lesson.
(iii) It helps the teacher to keep the teaching procedure and objectives in minds.
(iv) It ensures availability to necessary materials and saves last minute rush to provide adequate arrangements and anxiety caused by such a situation.
(v) It serves as an aid for future plans.

Essentials of a Good Lesson Plan

A good lesson plan should

(i) be prepared shortly before use.
(ii) be specific and detailed.
(iii) take cognizance of individual differences.
(iv) include (a) statement of objectives of the lesson; (b) statement of activities and experiences with instructional points; (c) a list of materials needed; (d) description of method and procedures to be used; (e) provisions for linking previous and future plans; (f) provisions for comments by the teacher after the lesson.

Whatever the type of method selected for teaching it should be compatible with the purpose or desired outcome and the best among available methods to bring the desired outcome. It should be adapted to the activity to be taught. It should also be feasible taking into consideration time, space and equipment available. The teacher should have the skill to use a particular method. Proper orientation and understanding of the techniques and purpose of the method should be given to the students.

The immediate goal of any yogic lesson is to introduce a particular yoga practice and its correct technique and give the feel of that practice of the participants of the lesson so that they are motivated to do further practice and derive maximum benefits. In order to attain these objectives the yogic lesson should be properly planned and executed.

Guidelines for Conducting Yoga Lessons Successfully

1. *Setting the Atmosphere*: A yoga class should begin with a calm and quiet atmosphere. It may start with a short prayer or with a transquil mood. As far as possible some meditative pose may be recommended for this purpose. The students are asked to take their seats in a suitable formation. The quiet sitting or meditative tone creates suitable internal environment in the students conducive to the yoga lesson.

2. *Introduction to the Practice*: The main part of the lesson starts with the introduction of the yoga practice. This introductory part may be divided into two sections. The first part may be devoted to verbal instructions with the back-ground of the practice containing as much information about the practice as possible. This part is specially intended to create interest and motivation among the students. Depending upon the knowledge of the teacher about the practice and his/her skill in presenting the information, the teacher can make this more interesting and motivating.
3. *Demonstrating Practice*: The second part may be devoted to the ideal demonstration of the yoga practice as a whole. Although it is possible to take the help of Audio-visual aids like pictures, sketches, filmstrips etc., it is more impressive, practical and desirable that the demonstration is staged by the teacher himself. As far as possible this demonstration should be most efficient, faultless and complete so that an overall image of the practice is presented to the students. As compared to the presentation of a particular yoga practice through an audio-visual means, when the teacher himself demonstrates the practice the students can relate personally to the teacher his own experiences and identify more closely with the practices shown. There is more appreciation and respect for the teacher generated through live demonstration.
4. *Analysing the Practice*: The whole demonstration of the yoga practice may be useful in forming an overall general picture. But is may not be enough to get into the detailed stages of the technique which requires analysis of that practice. The insight into the proper technique is gained only be analysing the practice is more essential when the technique is difficult.

   When the practice is simple a demonstration as a whole would be sufficient and the analysis may not be necessary. When the practice is analysed and demonstrated in parts, it is desirable to supplement it with a brief and clear description about the technique, bringing to the notice of the students salient points of the practice. These salient points should include hints about do's and don'ts.
5. *Students' Individual Practice Time*: When students see a technique demonstrated, they naturally want to try it out themselves. So allot some time for the students to try it on their own individually and to find out for the students to try it on their own individually and to find out for themselves how successfully they are able to practice it.

   While students are practicing the teacher should watch their performance and find out their difficulties, mistakes and deviations from the correct and ideal performance of the practice. He should correct the most obvious mistakes of those students who are practicing in a way that is detrimental to them and then point out common mistakes that are committed generally. A repeat demonstration of the practice as a whole and in parts should be given to ensure that the point of the corrections has been understood by everyone.

6. *Group Practice*: After getting the feel of the practice and becoming conversant with the technique the teacher may ask the whole group of students to perform the practice together under the guidance of the teacher in a formal manner. Collective participation in the group will give an idea to the individual about his performance in relation to the performance of others.
7. *Correcting Mistakes*: Performance in the group by te students helps the teacher to locate any performance that has deviated from normal and which needs correction. This saves the time of the teacher in checking every individual's performance. He can concentrate on the particular students who are not performing the technique properly. He can suggest necessary modifications in the performance of the students or suggest some lead-up practices in case of particular individuals, if necessary. Yoga practices being essentially individualistic, when they are performed by the group, individual capacities should be taken into consideration.
8. *Giving Instructions*: In the group practice when directions are used, it should be remembered that their purpose is to suggest different stages of practice to be undergone in succession by the group. The commands or instructions should, therefore, have a very slow rhythm so that the jerky motions in response to brisk instructions ar5e avoided and due respect is given to the individual capacities. The emphasis should be on an informal way of performance rather than a formal one.
9. *Repeat Demonstration*: The performance of the yoga practice by the group should be followed by pointing out the lacunae still remaining in the performance of some individuals, suggesting proper corrections and avoiding the mistakes committed by the individuals and elaborating on some points which need clarification or explanation.
10. *Repeat Practice*: The group should then repeat the practice of the technique.
11. *Repeat Demonstration*: The teacher should demonstrate and clarify the main points again.
12. *Rest Periods*: After the group practice is over the students may be given rest in the form of Shavasana—the yogic way of relaxation. When more than one yoga practice is introduced, it is desirable that Shavsana is practiced at the end of the lesson and sometimes even after some yoga practices during the lesson, if necessary.

Before the end of the lesson the teacher would do well to sum up points considered as important for the correct and efficient performance of yoga practices. He could also induce students to ask any questions related to the practice so that there is a good imprint the introduced yoga practice on the memory of the students.

To sum up the precise steps in the conduct of a yogic lesson, the whole process includes—

1. Creating an environment suitable for the lesson by a prayer or prayerful mood.
2. Establish the concept of yoga practice by verbal introduction.
3. Giving the complete picture of the yoga practice through whole demonstration.
4. Analaysing the whole performance into suitable parts or stages.
5. Allotting time for getting the feel of the practice by individuals.
6. Group practice under the guidance and supervision of the teacher.
7. Detection and correction of the mistakes in the performance.
8. Giving instructions with emphasis on the salient points analysing the performance again.
9. Giving complete demonstration with clear explanation of the various stages involved in the practice.
10. Practice by the group.
11. Again providing complete picture of the whole practice by demonstration, discussion, modifications when necessary, lead up practices for weaker students.
12. Giving complete rest in Shavasana at the end.

Success of the teacher lies in how best he utilizes the above steps in his lesson, Remember, "Teaching is what you make it". The above mentioned ideas or considerations relate to the yoga lesson where new practice is introduced. But a yoga lesson could also be a practice session. Previously introduced practices are undergone during such a lesson. There would obviously be some difference between the two types of yoga lessons. The main purpose of the first type of lesson would be to teach new practice with all details of its technique. The second type, on the other hand emphasizes the continuing practice of those techniques already learnt, so that the original techniques are not forgotten and their appropriate health benefits are derived. In the practice type of yoga lesson,

(i) there are groups of yogic practices undergone;
(ii) the practices are meaningfully chosen from amongst the known techniques;
(iii) there is some sequence based on the principle of progression; and

(iv) as far as possible variety of the groups of yogic practices are chosen for giving maximum benefits through stretching, relaxation, breathing techniques and meditation.

The practice lesson should also follow the pattern given earlier, where the lesson begins with a calm and quiet mood and ends with general relaxation with Shavasana or meditation, so that the ultimate experience is given to the participants in the lesson. A yoga lesson could be also a mixture of the above two types. After having conducted a practice lesson for some time, the teacher could switch into the introduction of the new practice along a similar pattern to the one discussed earlier. Emphasis in advanced groups in practice session could be on a meditative mood throughout the lesson or more time could be devoted to practice of meditation at the end.

Conducting a Lesson on Meditation

"Meditation is a mental device that limits stimulus input by directing attention to a single unchanging or repetitive stimulus". Throughout recorded history it has been used to alter state of consciousness. It forms a part of religious practices. Recently Meditation has been used for therapeutic purposes rather than as a religious practice. Meditation can be used as a noncultic practice. The technique of Meditation is related to the biofeedback techniques and to the relaxation methods.

Characteristics of Meditation

1. During meditation one gets profound rest for the body and mind, Oxygen consumption can be lowered during 20-30 minutes of meditation to a degree which can be reached after 6-7 hours of sleep.
2. Heart and respiratory rates typically decrease.
3. There is a shift to parasympathetic dominance.
4. There is a lowering of anxiety at this time.
5. During Meditation EEG shows an alert-drowsy pattern with high alphs and occasional theta wave patterns as well as unusual pattern of swift shifts from alpha to slower (more sleep-like) frequencies and then back again.
6. Meditation has been physiologically termed as 'wakeful, hypometabolic state'.
7. When practiced regularly it appears that Meditation alters behaviour suggesting number of beneficial changes.

Cautions

Meditation has its limitations. All persons cannot practice meditation for 20 to

30 minutes. Overdose of meditation for such persons can be dangerous. The theory of "More the better" cannot be applied here. Release of certain emotions that is difficult to handle may occur with prolonged meditation. In a person with an adverse psychiatric history, the beginning of meditation has been known to precipitate psychotic episodes. Even in relatively stable people, it is probably unwise to introduce prolonged sessions of meditation. To avoid such difficulties meditation should be practiced in moderation. It would be beneficial to start the practice of meditation after some amount of practice in stretchings like Asanas, rhythmic breathing like Pranayama and relaxative techniques like Shavasana.

It is doubtful whether meditation can really be ever taught effectively. In fact the state of meditation results out of the background prepared through variety of means contributing to a "meditative mood" which lasts not too long.

The Method of Teaching Meditation

The method of teaching meditation, therefore, requires creating an atmosphere of tranquility through pleasant voice and simple techniques leading to a meditative mood.

All the yogic practices contribute to the building up of the meditative mood. Rather than introducing mechanical technique of meditation the participants be brought to "meditative mood" and left there for a comfortable time, the time being determined by the individual according to his capacity. It is therefore desirable that meditation should be introduced along with the group of yogic practices rather than as an isolated technique, so that it becomes more beneficial and less harmful. It should be remembered that in the hierarchy of yogic practices meditation occupies a higher position than other practices. However, all yogic practices are complementary to each other and each practice contributes to similar effects on a greater or a lesser scale. Stable, comfortable and erect sitting with head, neck and trunk in a vertical line and regulated breathing facilitates the practice of meditation.

EVALUATION IN YOGA TEACHING

In the education system, the term evaluation is associated with examination, stress and anxiety. All efforts at curriculum definition and renewal come to naught if they cannot engage with the bulwark of the evaluation and examination system embedded in teaching. A good evaluation and examination system can become an integral part of the learning process and benefit both the learners themselves and the educational system by giving credible feedback. This chapter addresses Evaluation in Yoga Teaching as they are relevant as the normal course of teaching-learning, as a part of the system.

Yoga Education is concerned with preparing citizens for a meaningful and productive life, and evaluation should be a way of providing credible feedback on the extent to which we have been successful in imparting such an education. Seen from this perspective, current processes of evaluation, providing feedback on scholastic and academic development, can be achieved only if the Yoga teacher is prepared even before the course of teaching begins, armed with not only the techniques of assessment but also the parameters for evaluation and the various tools that will be employed.

In addition to judging the quality of the Yoga teacher it is necessary to collect, analyze and interpret their performances on various measures of the assessment to come to an understanding of the extent and nature of the students' learning in different domains. The purpose of assessment is necessarily to improve the teaching-learning process and materials, and to be able to review the objectives that have been identified for different school stages by gauging the extent to which the capabilities of learners have been developed.

There are many areas of the curriculum that can be assessed for which we still do not have reliable and efficient instruments. This includes assessing learning that is carried out in groups, and learning in areas such as multimedia presentation, demonstration and lecture where skills and competencies develop over longer time scales and require careful observation.

There are several points where we can assess the performance of a Yoga Teacher, among them few are important: Subject knowledge expert, Self disciplined, Language command, Flow of voice, Understanding of the student's mentality, Learning tendency, Sincerity, Regularity, Punctuality, Politeness, Creative and above all Dedication over the Stream of Yoga. Of course all these point cannot be assessed easily at a time so continuous evaluation process can be adopted here in Yoga Teacher Evaluation.

Well-designed assessment and regular report cards provide learners with feedback, and set standards for them to strive towards. They also serve to inform about the quality of learning and the development and progress of their wards. This is not a means of encouraging competition; if one is looking for quality in Yoga education, then segregating and ranking them with feelings of inferiority will develop so cannot do it.

Yoga teachers require specific training by their Educators for effective training that can be of assistance in remediation efforts. Firstly we should start the evaluation keeping the first sutra of Patanjali in mind:

> *Atḥa Ỵogāṇuśāsanam*
>
> —Yoga Sutra 1/1

Meaning: now therefore the disciplines of Yoga. As the Yoga Sutra starts with discipline, thus every aspirant of yoga need to have this quality deep rooted in his behaviour. If this single quality is there, one can gain the other required quality of a good Yoga Teacher.

Second point of evaluation of a Yoga teacher should be his sincerity, regularity, and punctuality, keeping the fourteenth sutra of Patanjali in mind:

Sa tu dirgha-käla-nairantarya-satkäräsevito dṛdha-bhümiḥ
—Yoga Sutra 1/14

Meaning: It becomes firmly grounded by being continued for a long time with reverence, without interruption. If this second quality is there in the aspirant, he is definitely going to be the master of his subject and afterwards he will be judged as a good yoga teacher.

As long as examinations and tests assess the ability of the learner, to remember and recall textbook knowledge, all attempts to redirect the curriculum towards learning will be thwarted. First, tests in knowledge-based subject areas must be able to gauge what aspirant have learnt, and their ability to use this knowledge for problem solving and application in the real world. In addition, they must also be able to test the processes of thinking to gauge if the learner has also learnt where to find information, how to use new information, and to analyze and evaluate the same.

Continuous and comprehensive evaluation has frequently been cited as the only meaningful kind of evaluation. This also requires much more careful thinking through about when it is to be employed in a system effectively. Such evaluation places a lot of demand on teachers' time and ability to maintain meticulous records if it is to be meaningfully executed and if it is to have any reliability as an assessment. If this simply increases stress on children by reducing all their activities into items for assessment, or making them experience the teacher's 'power', then it defeats the purpose of education. Unless a system is adequately geared for such assessment, it is better for teachers to engage in more limited forms of evaluation, but incorporating into them more features that will make the assessment a meaningful record of learning.

Preparing report cards is a way for the educator to know about each individual what she/he has learnt during the term, and what she/he needs to work on and improve. To be able to write such report cards, educator would need to think about each individual, and hence pay attention to them during their everyday teaching and interaction. One does not need special tests for this; learning activities themselves provide the basis for such ongoing observational and qualitative assessments of children. Maintaining a daily diary based on observation helps in continuous and comprehensive evaluation.

Areas that Require Fresh Thinking

The belief that assessment must lead to finding learning difficulties to them be remediated is often very impractical and not founded on a sound understanding of pedagogic practice. Problems regarding conceptual development cannot and do not wait for formal tests in order to be detected. A teacher can, in the course of teaching itself, come to know of such problems by asking questions that make learner think or by giving them small assignments. He or she can then attend to them in the process of teaching-by ensuring that her planning is flexible and responsive to the learners and their learning.

Every classroom interaction between Yoga teacher and Educator requires their evaluation of their own work, and a discussion with them about what should be tested and the ways of finding out whether the competencies are being developed or not. Even many newcomers are able to give correct assessments of what they can or cannot do well. The role of teaching is to provide an opportunity to each individual to learn to the best of his or her ability and provide learning experiences that develop cognitive qualities.

Assessment at Different Stages

Beginners Stage: At this stage, assessment must be purely qualitative. Judgments of Yoga teacher activities in various domains and an assessment of the status of their basic interests and development, based on observations through everyday interactions. On no account should they be made to take any form of test, oral or written.

Elementary Stage: A variety of methods may be used, including oral and written tests and observations. The Yoga Teacher should be aware that they are being assessed, but this must be seen by them as a part of the teaching process and not as a fearful constant threat. Grades or marks along with qualitative judgments of achievement and areas requiring attention are essential at this stage. Their own self-evaluation can also be a part of the report card. Rather than examinations, there could be short tests from time to time, which are criterion based.

Higher Stage: Assessment may be based more on tests, examinations and project reports for the knowledge-based areas of the curriculum, along with self-assessment. Other areas would be assessed through observation and also through self-evaluation.

IX

Yoga Practices

COMMON INSTRUCTIONS FOR THE PRACTICE

Maharśi Patanjali begins his Yogic text with the Sutra "***Athayogānuśāsanam***" which indicates that Yoga needs a discipline. There are various paths to Yoga but in the context where one starts for health and fitness he should understand one thing very clearly that he cannot achive the advanced postures in a few days; the perfection needs long practice, which can be attain through the preliminary practices like joints loosening practices. The preleminry practices make the muscles and joints flexible enough so that the aspirant can attain the advance postures.

Begin the yogic practice with few defined disciplines like: select a clean and well ventilated place for yogic practices. Better to sit on a blanket or carpet. Early morning is the best time. However, they can be performed in the evening. For the practices dress should be loose, not very tight

Firstly pray to God mentally, you to bestow the strength follow the rights path. Better to chant 'OM' thrice to make the mentality subline. After that chant Gayatri Mantra. Remember the Guru and pray for his subtle protection. After that start the practices.

Gayatri Mantra:

"Om bhūrbhuvah swah tatsaviturvarenyam
bhargo devasya dhimahi dhiyo yo nah prachodayāt"

(May Almighty illuminate our intellect and inspire us towards the righteous path)

With regular practice of a balanced series of techniques, the energy of the body and mind can be liberated and the quality of consciousness can be expanded. This is not a subjective claim but is now being investigated by the scientists and being shown by an empirical fact. Over time, the benefits of

Yoga practice have a cumulative effect, improving the well-being of the practitioner.

With every group of practice there are special instructions by the author given in the beginning of the chapters, through which an aspirant can adopt the Yogic discipline easily or a Yoga instructor can just repeat the instruction to his disciple comfortably.

Fig. 1: Initial Position

PREPARATORY PRACTICES

There are several practices that can be introduced before Yoga practice and it varies from School to School. Here we introduce the set of fourteen practices which come under Joints loosening practices. These practices include almost all movement of our joints which is beneficial for the muscle's and joint's flexibility. This comes under preliminary practice of Asana. It includes the physical movement, mental awareness and pranic flow all together. In this way it not only gives a massaging effect on our body but also improves the blood circulation as well. It eliminates the wastes from our body, and that's why these practices reduce the joints pain as well as the rheumatic problems. It improves the blood circulation also due to that we observe a positive impact on blood pressure and cardiovascular disorders. There are several other benefits also so one should must go through this set of practice.

1. *Pādanguli Naman*: Sit with the legs out stretched and give the support of hands keeping them beside the buttocks. Start moving your toes, only toes not the feet or ankle. With inhalation open them and with exhalation fold. Very slowly repeat the practice five times and then sit quietly for a moment. Observe the effects of the practice. Feel the pain and stretch in feet region.

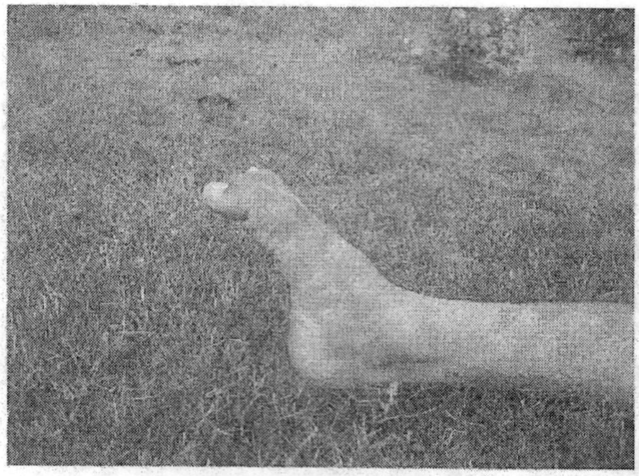

Fig. 2: Padanguli Naman

2. *Gulf Naman*: Be in the same position; now start moving the ankle-forward and backward. Keep the toes static. While stretching the ankle out side inhale and while bringing it back exhale. All your awareness should be on the ankle region. Observe the effects after completing the five rounds. Feel the pain and pressure given in the ankle region.

Fig. 3: Gulfnaman

3. *Gulf Ghūrnan*: Fold the left leg and keep it on the next thigh. Grasp the left ankle with left hand and the feet region with right hand. Now start rotating your ankle with the help of hand five times clockwise and five anticlockwise. Repeat the practice with right leg. Sit quietly for a moment; observe the effect of this practice in knee region, calf muscle, ankle region and the feet. All the related muscles and tendons have been stretched and activated. Feel the pranic flow and better blood circulation as well as the stiffness being released from this region.

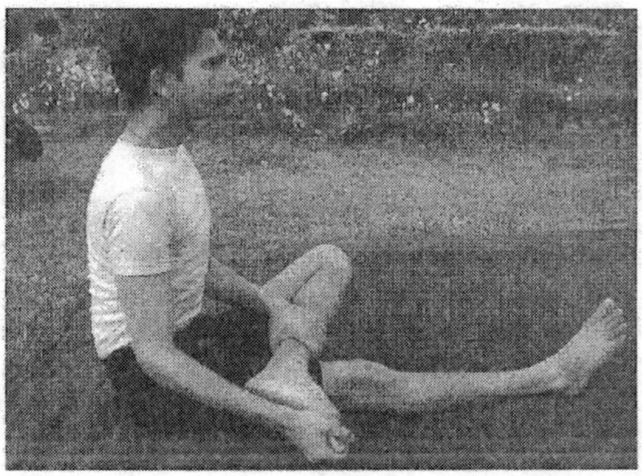

Fig. 4: Gulf Ghūrnan

4. *Jānu naman*: Lock your hands under the left thigh now; start moving the knee with the help of hands. Exhale while bending the knee and inhale while stretching it out. Be aware that the heel should not touch the floor. With full awareness stretch it fully while opening the knee; bring it closer to the chest while bending the knee. After completing the five rounds start the same practice with right leg. Sit with the eyes closed, and observe the effect of this practice.

Fig. 5: Janunaman

5. *Jānu Chakra*: Lock your hands under the left thigh up to elbow level. Start rotating the leg with knee joint. Inhale while bringing the leg up and after completing a big circle bring it down with exhalation. Repeat it five times clockwise and five times anti clockwise. After completing the rounds do the same with right leg. Now sit quietly for a moment and observe the effects of this practice; feel the stretch in thigh and calf muscle; feel the pain in hip and knee joint; feel the pressure at abdominal muscles.

Fig. 6: Janu Chakra

6. *Jānu Falak Akarśan*: Again sit in the base position (with legs out stretched); start contracting the muscles of thigh just above the knees. Repeat it five times with the both legs. Practice is highly effective for the people suffering with knee pain.

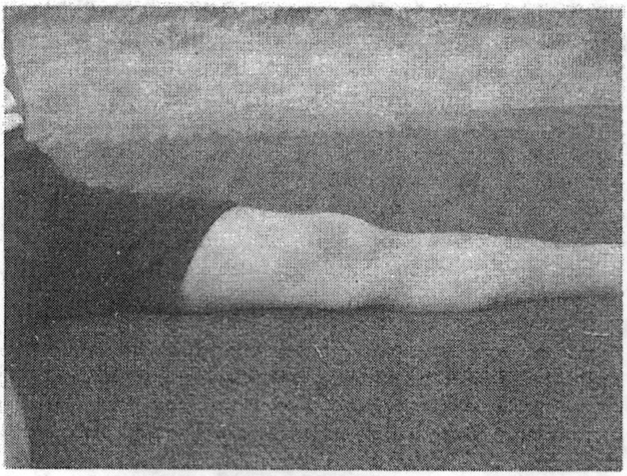

Fig. 7: Janu Falak Akarsan

7. *Ardhtatali*: Again fold the left knee and keep it over the thigh. Keep right hand on the foot and grasp the knee with left. Start up and down movement of it and feel the hip joint is being opened. Repeat it slowly at least five times and do the same with right leg.

Fig. 8: Ardhatitali

8. Pūrnatitali: Bring both the sole closer and lock the feet with hands over it. Now start moving the knees up and down as like a butter fly. Be aware that the spine should be erect and chest opened. Sit quietly after few rounds. Observe the opening of the hip joint, stretch out the hamstring muscles, feel all the effect of this practice.

Fig. 9: Purnatitali

9. *Śroni Chakra*: Again sit like the practice of arthatitli; this time rotate the knee so that hip joint may be rotating five times clock wise five anti clock. After completing the practice repeat with the right leg. The practice is helpful to people who cannot sit cross legged.
   Note: Sit in vajrasana for further practices with knee bended and buttocks on the heels. If it is difficult for a long time adopt any cross legged posture while keeping the spine erector legs out stretched.

Fig. 10: Shronichakra

10. *Mustikā Bandha*: Raise the hands up to shoulder level; keep the elbow strait. Make the fist tight while keeping the thumb inside with exhalation; open the fingers and palm with inhalation. Practice five times and then observe the effect of the practice.

Fig. 11: Mustikabandh

11. *Manibandha Chakra*: Raise the hands while tightening the fist. This time rotate the wrist in clock wise and anti-clock wise direction separately. Rest for a moment and observe the effect of this practice. Feel the stretch in lower arm, wrist, palm and fingers. Feel better blood circulation and better flow of prana in these regions.

Fig. 12: Manibandh Chakra

12. *Kehuni Naman*: This time bend the elbows while bringing the hands on the shoulders; five times on ward and five times side ways direction. Inhale while opening the elbows, exhale while bending them.

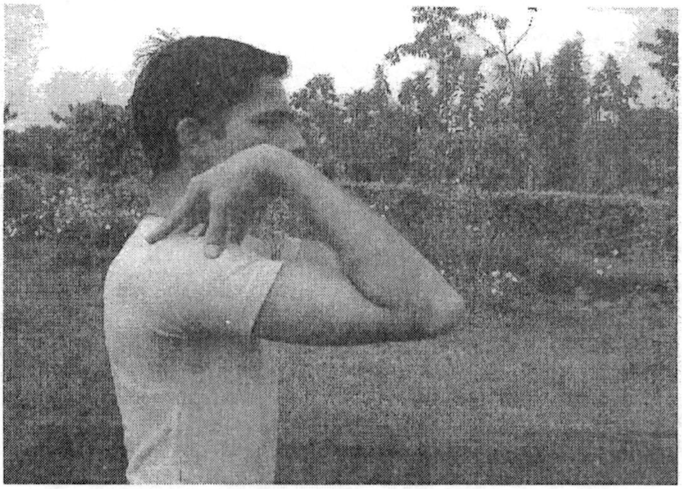

Fig. 13: Kehuni Naman

13. *Skandh Chakra*: Keep the elbows bended; rotate the shoulders while bringing the elbows back making a circle in inward and outward direction five times each. After completing the practice observe the effect. Feel the effect in the spine, shoulder blades, arms, elbows and the lower arms. Feel the removed stiffness from this region as well as better blood circulation and pranic flow.

Fig. 14: Skandhachakra

14. *Grīvā Sanchālan*: Start moving the neck. Firstly forward and backward with exhalation and inhalation; Next sideways bending with exhalation. Lastly rotate the neck. While bringing back inhale and bringing forward exhale. Rotate slowly in clock wise and anti clock wise direction. Practice should be slow and with full awareness. After completing the rounds sit quietly for a moment and observe the effect of these practices.

Fig. 15: Griva Sanchalan

SŪRYA NAMASKĀR

In daily life, Yoga helps a person to attain a relaxed state of mind. It provides thus vitality, vigor and zest to carry out his life. All negative blocks in the mind are removed. The body is cleansed of all the impurities and toxins.

Personal power is enhanced by the practice of yoga. One learns to identify his own inner resources and draws upon the energy needed from his own inner sources. It helps him to increase his awareness, i.e. self-awareness. It helps in attention focus and concentration.

The whole science of yoga has one view in common-to gain health, personal power, to develop knowledge and attain peace of mind. It also reduces stress and tension in the physical body and activates the parasympathetic nervous system.

Practice of Surya Namaskar includes twelve postures and helpful to the children, adolescent and the youth. It also includes the āsanas (postures) breath awareness and physical awareness. The advanced practitioners can add the mantras and chakra awareness also. Following Instructions can be followed by the practitioners for the practice:

Position One Pranāmāsana: Mantra ('Om Mitraye Namah') Raise the both hands and bring them in-front of the chest in praying position. The awareness should be at chest region (An āhat Chakra).

Fig. 16: Pranamasana

Position Two Hastotthānāsana: Mantra ('Om Ravaye Namah') Inhale and raise the hands above the head and tilt yourself little backward. Awareness at neck region (Viśuddhi Chakra).

Fig. 17: Hastotthānāsana

Position Three Padhastāsana: Mantra ('Om Sūryāy Namah') Exhale and bend the body with hips. Try to keep the palm beside the feet and touch the nose with knees. Awareness at hip joint (Swādhisthan Chakra).

Fig. 18: Padhastāsana

Position four Aśwāsanchālan: Mantra ('Om Bhānve Namah') Inhale and bring the left leg back with opening the chest and raising the head. Awareness at head region (Ajnā Chakra).

Fig. 19: Aśwāsanchālan

Position Five Dandâsana: Mantra ('Om Khagâye Namah') Exhale and bring the both legs back while making the body like stick giving the total weight on hands and legs. Awareness at abdominal region (Manipur Chakra).

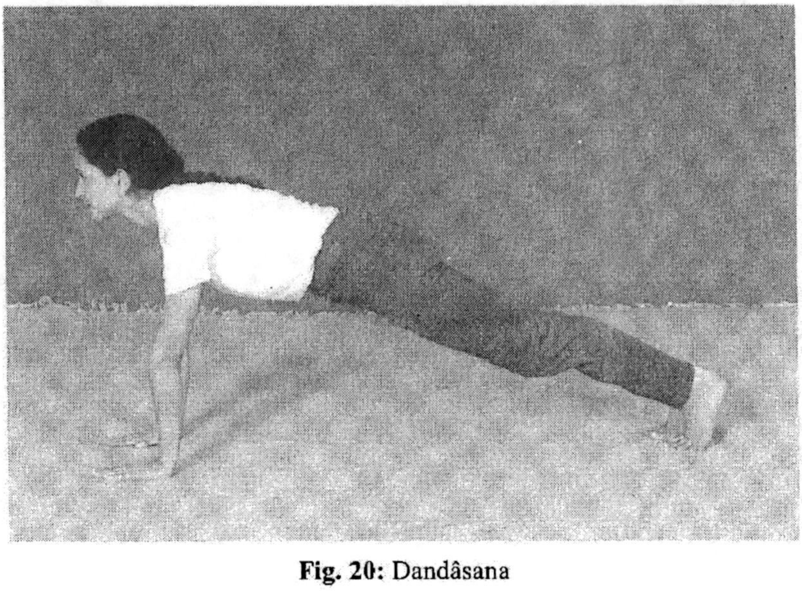

Fig. 20: Dandâsana

Position Six Astānga Namaskār: Mantra ('Om Puśne Namah') Holding the breath outside, keep the knees, chest and forehead on the floor. Lift the buttocks up. Awareness should be at chest region (Anāhat Chakra).

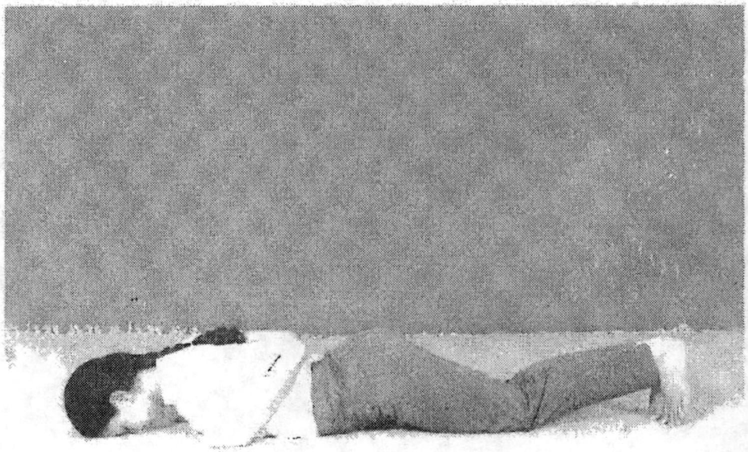

Fig. 21: Astānga Namaskār

Position Seven Bhujangāsana: Mantra ('Om Hiranyagarbhāy Namah') Inhale and raise the upper trunk of the body up while keeping the thigh on the floor. Awareness at hip joint (Swādhisthan Chakra).

Fig. 22: Bhujangāsana

Position Eight Parvatāsana: Mantra ('Om Mārichaye Namah') Exhale and raise hip and buttocks up while bringing the head down. Try to gaze at the navel and keep the heel on the floor. Awareness at the neck region (Viśuddhi Chakra).

Fig. 23: Parvatāsana

Position Nine Aśwasanchālana: Mantra ('Om Adityāye Namah') Inhale and bring the left leg forward between the both hands, coming back into the practice. Awareness at head region (Ajnā Chakra).

Fig. 24: Aśwasanchālana

Position Ten Padhastāsana: Mantra ('Om Śavitre Namah') hips forward while lifting the hips up into *Padhastāsana*. Awareness at hip joint (Swādhisthan Chakra).

Fig. 25: Padhastāsana

Position Eleven Hastotthānāsana: Mantra ('Om Arkāye Namah') Inhale and raise the both hands above the head and tilt the body back. Awareness at neck region (Viśuddhi Chakra).

Fig. 26: Hastotthānāsana

Position Twelfth Pranamāsana: Mantra ('Om Bhāskarāye Namah') Bring the both hands infront of the chest in praying position with exhalation. Awareness at chest region (Anāhat Chakra).

Fig. 27: Pranamasana

MEDITATIVE, CULTURAL AND RELAXATION ĀSANA

Uttānpādāsana: Lie flat on your back; keep the feet together, hands beside the body with palms facing downward. Raise the left leg (keeping the knee strait) with inhalation. Bring it down with exhalation. Repeat it five times. Do the same practise with the right leg. Be aware of the effects of the practise. Feel the stretch in thigh and calf muscle, feel the pressure on the abdominal muscles; feel the pain in hip and knee joints. After completing the rounds relax in śavāsana for few minutes and feel better blood circulation and better flow of prāna in the related organs.

Fig. 28: Uttānpādāsana

Pād Chakrāsana: Be in the same position. While keeping the knee straight lift your one leg; rotate it; make a circle as big as possible three times clock wise and three times anti clock wise. Do the same with other leg. With inhalation raise the leg up and with exhalation bring it down. After completing the rounds again observe the effects.

Fig. 29: Pād Chakrāsana

Pād Sanchālan: Starting position is again the same. This practice is like cycling. Firstly with the left leg five times forward movement, five times backward. Now the same with right leg forward and backward and lastly both legs alternate as if cycling. During the whole practise the breathing pattern will be normal. After completing the rounds observe the effect at the abdominal muscles and chest region, thighs, knees, calf muscles and the whole lower part of the body.

Fig. 30: Pād Sanchālan

Pād Sanchālan: Fold both your knees and lock the hands over it. Inhale and with exhalation raise the head, neck and chest. Try to touch the nose with knees. Practice three to four times and relax in śavāsana.

Fig. 31: Pawanmuktāsana

Udarākarśan: Lock your hands under the head, fold your knees and keep closer to the chest. Exhale and twist the spine. Tilt the neck to the left and knees to the right. Inhale and come into centre. Exhale and twist to the reverse direction - neck to the right and knees to the left. Try to give a gentle massage to the spine. The practice activates the pancreas and other abdominal organs. It regulates digestion and helps proper functioning of the organs.

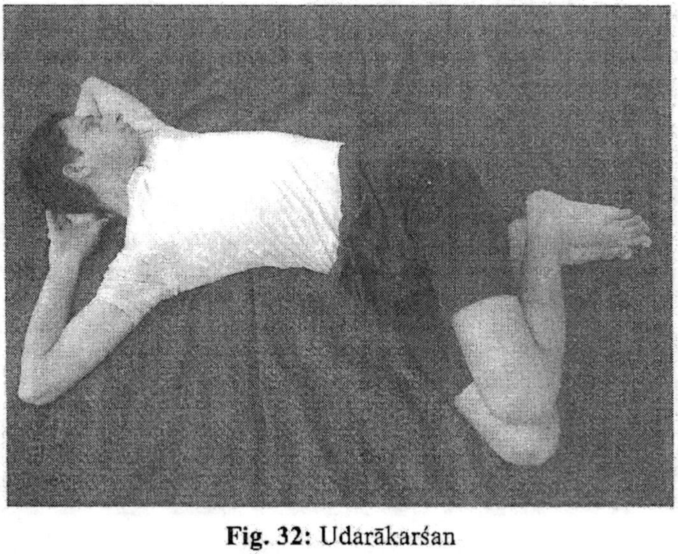

Fig. 32: Udarākarśan

Pristha Sanchālan: Come into the position of Pawanmuktāsana. Fold the knees and lock the hands over it. Sit in a squotting position and pawan-muktasana. Keep the breath normal and give the massage to the whole back from neck to buttocks. After completing the 10-12 rounds lie flat in śavasana. Observe the effect of this practice.

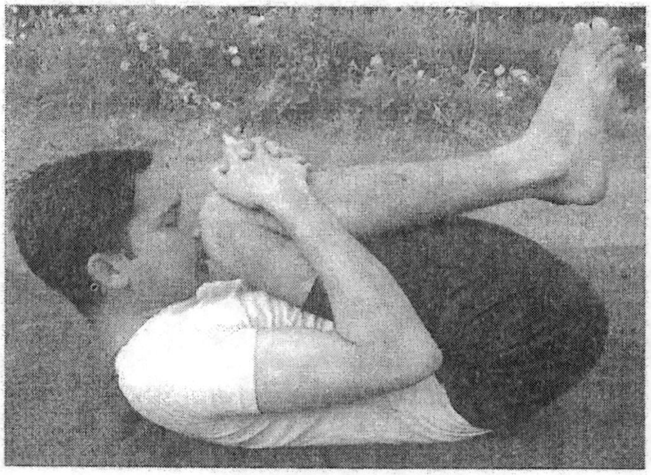

Fig. 33: Pristha Sanchālan

Chakki Chālāsana: Sit in the base position with the leg out stretched and separated. Look the hands and keep the elbows straight. Rotate the upper part of the body with hip joint just like churning a mill. Exhale and bend forward while touching the both toes with the hands; while making a circle inhale and band backward. Five times clockwise and five times anti clockwise. During the practice the elbows should remain straight. After completing the rounds relax for some moment and observe the effects. Feel the pressure at abdominal muscles the pain in hip and knee joint and the stretch in thigh and calf muscle. Feel gentle pain in arms.

Fig. 34: Chakki Chālāsana

Naukachālāsana: Sit in base position with legs together. Make the fist like something heavy in your hand. Make the movement of the body like boating-forward and backward. While raising the hands and bringing it back. Inhale during bringing the upper trunk back and exhale during bending forward. Practice 3-5 rounds. Sit quietly for few seconds and observe the effects of the practice.

Fig. 35: Naukachālāsana

Kāsthatakśanāsana: Sit into the scooting position with legs little separated. Inhale and raise the both hands together like having an axe in the hands, and make the fist. Exhale and produce 'hah' soundand bring the hands suddenly down just like chopping the wood. Practice 5-10 rounds feeling that you are exhaling all the negative emotions like anger and fear. Sit quietly for some moment observe the calmness of the mind and feel the energy and positive emotions.

Fig. 36: Kāsthatakśanāsana

Tādāsana: Come into standing position with legs together. Lock the hands over the head while palm turning upward. Concentrate on one point at eyelevel. Inhale and raise the heel and hands together. Give a good stretch to the body. Raise the heel and hands together, exhale and come into starting position. Practice five rounds and observe the effects on the spine, abdominal and chest region, arms and shoulder blades, thigh and calf muscles. After completing the rounds relax the arms, separate the legs and relax for a moment. Feel all the effects of this practice.

Fig. 37: Tādāsana

Tiryaktādāsana: Separate the legs and brings the hands in the position of tadasana. Inhale first, and during exhalation bend to the left, keeping the elbows strait. Come into centre with inhalation, again exhale and bend to the right. Do not give any jerk in the final position. Practice five rounds each side. Feel the effect in waist, shoulder blades, spinal cord and the whole trunk region.

Fig. 38: Tiryaktādāsana

Katichakrāsana: Separate the legs and raise the hands to the shoulder level with inhalation. Exhale and twist to the left. Bring the right hand on the left shoulder and the left hand to the back. Come into centre with inhalation. Twist to the right with exhalation. Practice five times each side. Feel the spinal twist and the abdominal massage. (After five rounds a normal person can practice it a bit fast for few rounds.

Fig. 39: Katichakrāsana

Siddhāsana: Sit with the legs out stretched. Fold the left knee and bring the heel of left leg at public floor (between anus and testis in male and at the cervix region in female). Now fold the right knee and bring the heel at pubic bone. Make the spine erect at the final position. Sit quietly for some moments with eyes closed. Practice is beneficial for spiritual awakening.

Fig. 40: Siddhāsana

Padmāsana: Sit with the legs outstretched first. Fold the left knee and bring the feet on the right thigh and the same with right leg. Bring the feet on left thigh. Keep the spine erect and sit with eyes closed for some moments. Practice is suitable for a long time meditation. It is also called the lotus pose.

Fig. 41: Padmāsana

Swastikasana: Sit with the legs out stretched. Fold the right knee and bring the soul of right leg touching with the left thie (between thie and calf muscles). Now fold the left knee and bring the soul between the thie and calf of right leg. Make the spine erect at the final position. Sit quietly for some moments with eyes closed. Practice is beneficial for spiritual awakening as discussed in Hath Yogic texts.

Fig. 42: Swastikasana

Sukhāsana: This one is the easiest pose in Yoga. Sukha literary means pleasure. The posture gives comfort as well as other spiritual benefits of meditative postures. Sit with the legs out stretched. Fold the right knee and bring the soul of under the left thie. Now fold the left knee and bring the under the (folded) right thie. Make the spine erect at the final position. Sit quietly for some moments with eyes closed. Practice is beneficial for spiritual awakening as discussed in Hath Yogic texts.

Fig. 43: Suḳhāsana

Paschimottānāsana: Sit with the legs outstretched toether. Inhale and raise the hands above the head. Strech up the upper part of the body. Exhale

Fig. 44: Paschimottānāsana

and bend yourself with hips. Try to lock the toes with first two fingers and keep the elbows on the floor. Try to touch the nose with the knees and lie the chest on the thighs. (Don't give any jerk in final position). Slowly inhale and raise the upper part of the body. It can be practiced with breath awareness in rounds. For the advance practitioner-hold the final position with normal breath for few seconds and increase the duration.

Dhanurāsana: Lie on your abdomen. Fold the knees and hold the ankles while bringing the hands back. Inhale and raise the head, chest, shoulders and the thigh and tense the knees. Hold the position as holding the breath for a moment. Exhale and come back into base position. (For the beginners it can be practiced for 2-3 rounds with breath awareness and for the advanced practitioners hold with the normal breathing in the final position according to capacity. Feel the effect of this practice for some moments.

Fig. 45: Dhanurāsana

Bhujangāsana: Lie on the abdomen bring the hands under the shoulders and palm facing downward. Inhale and raise the upper part of the body (head, shoulders and chest) try to gaze at the sky. Keep the elbows straight. Remember the thighs should touch the floor and legs should remain straight. Exhale and come into base position. For advanced practitioner—hold the position with normal breath. Observe the effects of this practice.

Fig. 46: Bhujangāsana

Ardhaśalabhāsana and Śalabhāsana: Lie on the abdomen. Bring the hands under the thighs and palm facing downward. Inhale and raise the left leg with knees straight. Hold the position for a moment. Feel the pressure and pain at hip region. Exhale and bring down the leg back on the floor. Repeat the practice with right leg. The practice called Ardhaśalabhāsana. For the advanced practitioner raise the both legs together and hold the position according to capacity. It is called Śalabhāsana.

Fig. 47: Śalabhāsana

Naukāsana: Lie flat on your back-while feet together and hands beside the body with palm facing downward. Now bring the palms over thighs. Inhale and lift the head chest, arms, hands, legs and thighs upto six inches up and hold the position for some moments. Suddenly leave all the body parts and let them come on the floor. During the final position only the buttocks and lower back will be remain on floor. Practice 3 rounds. Observe the effects on the abdominal muscles and whole body parts.

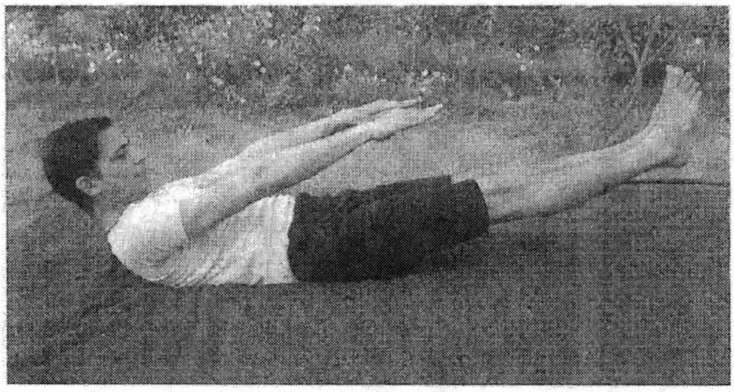

Fig. 48: Naukāsana

Mārjariāsana: Come into kneeling position and keep the hands one step forward like a found footed. The gap between hands will be approximate one foot and the gap between hands and knee will be one and a half feet. Inhale and raise the head; bend the neck back and the spine so that the back part of the body make small pit. Exhale- and raise the spine up and bend the neck forward so that abdominal muscles will make a pit. The practice activates nervous system and the blood circulation in the spinal region.

Fig. 49: Mārjariāsana

Simhāsana: Sit in Vajrāsana with knees separated; bring the hands under the thighs with you palm facing downward and fingers towards back. In this position the body will tilt little forward. Inhale and with the exhalation open the mouth, bring the tongue outside, make the sound like a lion is roaring and at the same time gaze bring your eyebrows together. Practice- 3 to 5 rounds and after completing the rounds and observe the effects.

Fig. 50: Simhāsana

Gomukhāsana: Sit with the legs out stretched. Fold the left knee and bring the heel beside the right buttock. Fold the right knee crossing over the left and bring the heel beside the left buttock. Try to keep the knees together. Now bring the right hand while crossing the head back and the left hand crossing the chest-lock both the hands or try for it. Hold the position for a moment and slowly release. Repeat the same with other side.

Fig. 51: Gomukhāsana

Vipreet karnee āsana: Lie flat on your back with legs together and palms closer to the body on the floor. Inhale and raise the both legs together, suddenly lift the buttocks and give the support of hands under hips. Hold the position with normal breath. Slowly release the position while folding the hip joints and bring the body in Śavāsana.

Fig. 52: Vipreet karnee āsana

Sarvāngāsana: Lie flat on your back with legs together and hands beside the buttocks and palm facing downward. Inhale and lift the legs, buttocks and hips together and give the support of hands to the back so that body may become vertical to the floor. Hold the position with normal breath. Slowly release the position with bringing the legs above the head. Slowly bring one by one vertibra on the floor. Relax for a moment in śavâsana and observe the effect of this practice.

Fig. 53: Sarvāngāsana

Natrājāsana: Stand with the legs together and gaze at one point at eye level. Raise the left hand above the head. Fold the right knee and hold the ankle with the same hand. Exhale and bend yourself with hip-joint while the left hand will come to the shoulder level. Hold the position; release and repeat with other side.

Fig. 54: Natrājāsana

Śavāsana: Lie flat on your back, separate the legs approximate one and half feet and bring the hands beside the body with the palm facing upward. Head, neck and spine should be in one line; eyes and lips gently closed. Inhale deeply and with every exhalation make yourself relaxed. Try to relax the whole body as well as the mind. Observe the whole body being on the floor. Rotate the consciousness on body parts and relax one-by-one. Relax the right hand fingers, palm, wrist, forearm, elbow, arm and shoulder, the right hand relaxed. Relax the left hand-fingers, palm, and wrist, forearm, elbows arm and shoulder, the left hand relaxed.

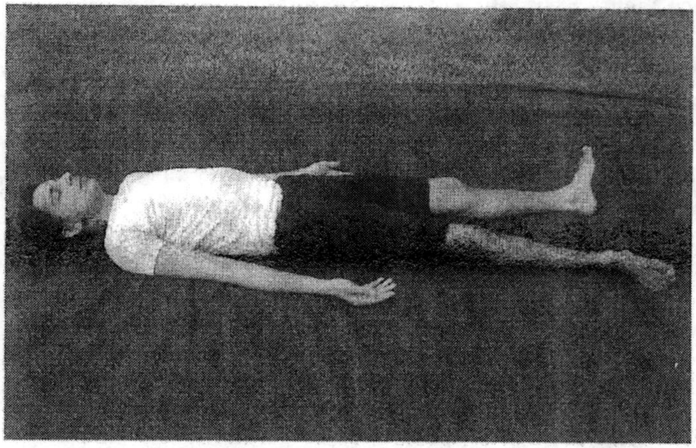

Fig. 55: Śavāsana

Relax the right leg—toes, sole, heel, foot, ankle, calf muscle, knee, thigh and right leg. Relax the left leg-toes, soul, heel, foot, ankle, calf muscle, knee, thigh, and left leg. Relax your, trunk both the buttocks, hip joint, abdomen, chest, back and, the whole trunk region. Relax the head region the neck, back of the head, top of the head, the forehead, the face and the whole head region. Now observe the breath. No change into breathing pattern, count down the breath from any number and slowly come up to zero.

Now observe the body and mind; slowly start moving the toes and fingers; move the hands, legs and neck. Turn to the left and come up slowly. Śavāsana ends.

PRĀNĀYĀMA PRACTICE

In Yoga, we seek to sustain and enhance the life force as much as possible absorbing as much ***Prana*** through breath. The most significant way of doing this is through the practice of pranayama (breathing techniques or breath control). ***Yama*** is translated as control, discipline, regulation or mastery. Hence, some translate pranayama as "breath control." *Ayama* is expansion, growth, extension, augmentation or magnification. Hence, another translation is "expansion of the life force." Both are loosely translated as "breath control," but realize that there is much more behind this definition. Pranayama is the fourth part of the eight-fold Yoga described in the Yogasutra of Patanjali. The credit for making the practice of pranayama popular as a discipline in its own right and as a means for maintaining the health of the body and mind goes to the followers of HathaYoga. They gave it a place of great importance among the practices of HathaYoga, and it was they who described various techniques of pranayama, emphasizing the utility of each of them. There are instructions to practice them saperately and comfortably.

Nādiśodhan: Adopt any comfortable meditative posture simply by sitting cross legged, Padmāsana or Sidhāsana with spine erect. Relax the body and close the eyes. Observe the natural breath.

Bring the right hand's index and middle finger between the eyebrows while thumb and ring finger will be on the nostrils. With the help of the thumb, close the right nostril and the ring finger to close the left.

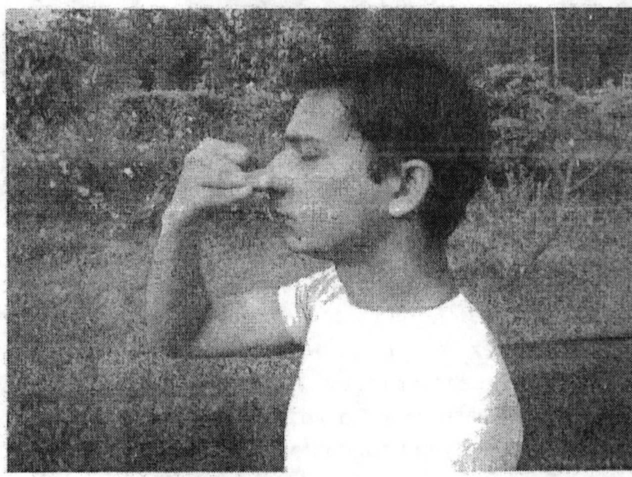

Fig. 56: Nādiśodhan

For the Beginners: Now inhale with the left nostril and exhale with the right. After that, inhale with right and exhale with left. The timing should be equal of inhalation and exhalation. Breath will be slow and steady.

For Advanced Practitioner: Inhalation and exhalation will be same. Here retentions of breath will be added. Inhale with the left, hold the breath inside, exhale with the right, again inhale with the right hold the breath inside and exhale with the left. It completes one round. Here inhalation, retention and exhalation should be of equal duration. Start practice with five rounds. Slowly increase the rounds with more practice.

(Precaution: Hypertensive and those suffering with heart problem should not retain the breath.)

Bhrāmari: Adopt any meditative posture with your spine erect. Close your eyes and close the ear with the help of index finger. Inhale deeply and exhale slowly producing the sound like a bee. Try to observe the vibration on your head. Practice five round in the beginning, and increase the rounds with duration.

Fig. 57: Bhrāmari

Ujjai: Again adopt the meditative pose with spine erect and eyes closed. Contract the epiglottis so that the air passage may contract. Inhale slowly

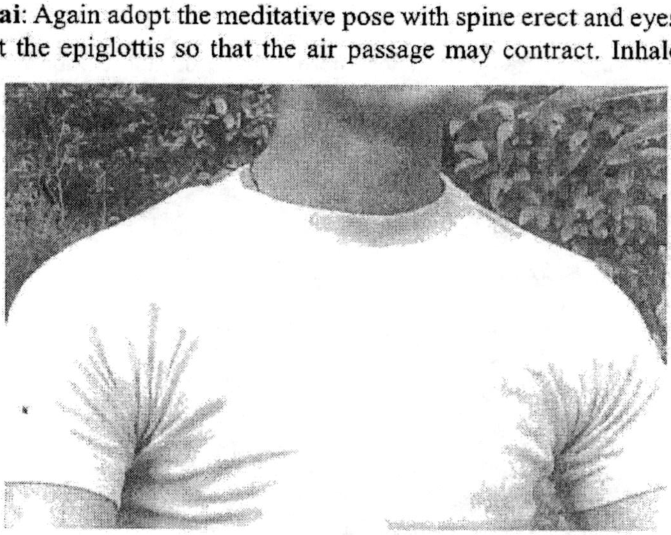

Fig. 58: Ujjai

with there tiny air passage while producing the hissing sound. According to capacity hold the breath with locking the chin into throat pit. Slowly exhale with same process unlocking the chin. Start the practice with five minutes and increase the duration with time being.

Sūryabhedan: Adopt any comfortable meditative posture again. Bring the hand on the nostrils. Inhale with the right and exhale with the left. For the beginners retention is not necessary. Continue the practice for few minutes. Practice a few rounds. The practice produces heat in your body (observe the effects).

Fig. 59: Sūryabhedan

Bhastrikā: In a meditative pose here, inhalation and exhalation should be rapid and sound producing. Practice five times and after that retain the breath. It completes one round. Practice according to capacity.

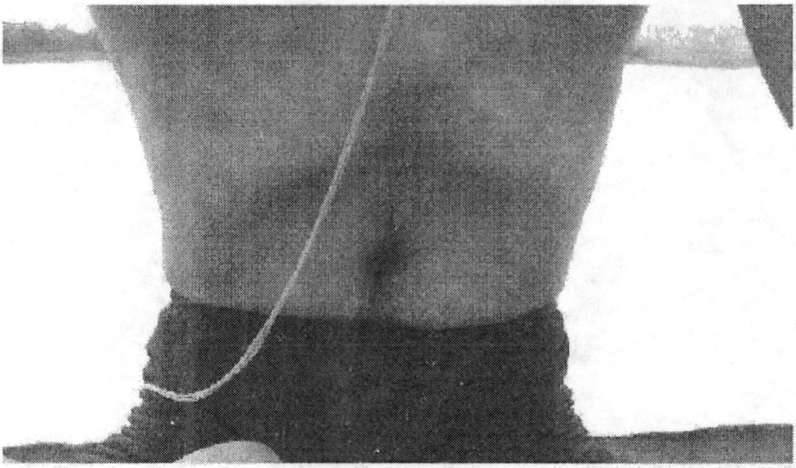

Fig. 60: Bhastrikā

Both the practices produces heat. Feel the energy in the body.

Śītali: In the meditative pose fold the tongue like a tiny pipe and the beak of crow. Inhale with this pipe and exhale with nostrils.

Fig. 61: Śītali

Śītkāri: For those who can't fold the tongue, just open the lips with teeth closed. Inhale with the mouth and exhale with nostrils. Feel the coolness in the buccal cavity. Then, observe the cooling effect on body and mind both.

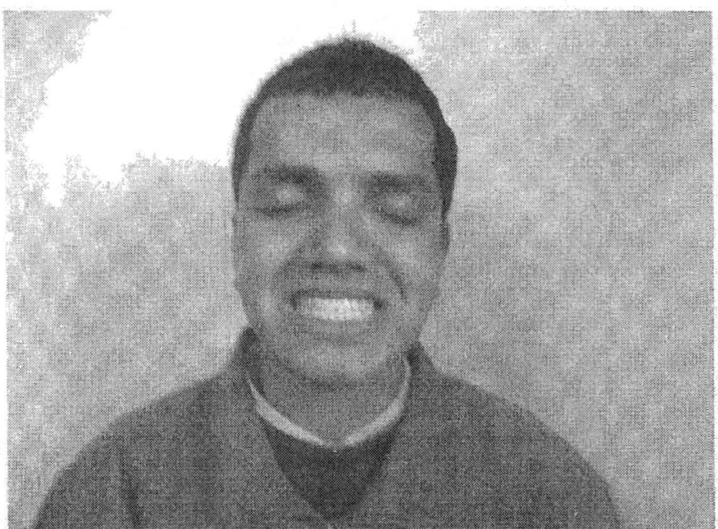

Fig. 62: Śītkāri

ŚATKARMA PRACTICE

Hatha Yoga is also known as the science of purification as it includes six types of cleansing process. In order to purify the mind it is necessary for the body as a whole to undergo a process of absolute purification. This purification or Śatkarma are: ***Dhauti, Neti, Basti, Nauli, Trataka*** and ***Kapalbhati***. Here is the brief of all six processes of Purification.

Neti

Neti cleans up the head and gives clairvoyance (Increases insight, sharpens perception). It also prevents all diseases which show themselves above the throat ("Hatha Yoga Pradipica" 2:30)

Thus, the benefits of Neti are much appreciated. Neti cleanses all nasal cavities washing out dust, small particles and old mucus that helps the even breathing. Neti cleanses the nasal diaphragms, rich with nerve endings. That helps the nose respond appropriately to the air we breathe. Neti stimulates, restores and toughens up all the ear-throat-nose system. Neti benefits the eyes by stimulating the tear channels and tear glands. The eyes become bright and shiny. Neti makes the head more clear and the voice much nicer. Neti practitioners gain better concentration and better memory. The face muscles become more relaxed, the skin of the face becomes smoother. As the air evenly

Fig. 63: Neti

flows through both nostrils, it equally stimulates both brain semi spheres, which brings harmony and balance to all body systems. The frontal segments of the brain responsible for higher mental abilities start functioning optimally. As a result, your intuition is improved and you develop creativity. Practice of Neti directly stimulates Ajna Chakra.

You need a Neti Pot, providing the spout is the right shape and size. It should be able to hold about a mug full of water, and you should be able to pour this water down your nostrils without splashing it over. Some people use a syringe.

Fill the warm salty water in neti pot. Check the nostril flow, which one is fluent? Set the tip of the pot at the same nostril. Breathe normally with the opened mouth. Till the neck little bit so that water may pass through one nostril to other.

Repeat the practice with the other nostril. After the practice of jalneti, Kapālbhāti is necessary—so that nostrils may become water free. Observe the effect of this practice. Feel the calmness of the mind.

Dhauti

Fig. 64: Dhauti

Dhauti is of several types but in practice commonly known as Kunjal or Vaman. "Vaman" means "vomiting" or "burp". Vaman Dhauti not only purifies stomach but using this technique, you can change direction of the Apana Vayu flow. Normally Apana Vayu flows downwards. Vaman Dhauti provokes it to flow upwards so that it brings a rejuvenative effect.

Fill a big pot (like jug) with warm salty water. Sit in scotting position and take the water more over capacity. Stand near a sink or a toilet. Drink fast 2 glasses of salty water. Lean forward, open the mouth and place the middle and index fingers on the back of the tongue as far as possible. Gently rub and press the back of the tongue. This should induce the water to gush out from the stomach. When the flow of water ceases, drink fast two more glasses of water and repeat the process. Continue vomiting until stomach is empty. After the practice lie down in śavāsana and observe the effect like emptiness of the stomach.

Laghū Sankha Prakśālana

It is the modified technique of Basti; keep approximate six glasses of warm-salty water in a jar. After taking two glasses of water, practice Tādāsana, Tiryaktādāsana, Katichakrāsana, Tiryakbhujangāsana and Udarākarśanāsana eight rounds each. Feel that the water is passing through the elementary canal.

Repeat the same process three times; you will feel the pressure of defecation. Excrete it out and relax in Śavāsana, the pressure may come again.

After forty five minutes of this practice, take khichari (The boiled rice and pulse with little salt without any other tastes).

Trātaka

Trataka eradicates all eye diseases, fatigue and sloth and prevents these problems". ("Hatha Yoga Pradipica" 2:31; 32) Trataka benefits not only the eyes but a whole range of physiological and mental functions. It is therapeutic in depression, insomnia, allergy, anxiety and postural problems. Not only that, further results of one-pointedness of the mind are strong willpower, improved memory and concentrative ability. Physiologically, Trataka relieves eye ailments such as eye strain and headache, myopia, astigmatism and even early stages of cataract. Trataka unlocks the inherent energy of the mind and channels it to the dormant areas of the unconscious. The eyes become clear bright, able to see the reality beyond appearances. This practice stimulates Ajna chakra and you develop telepathy, telekinesis, psychic healing and so on.

Trataka is a deceptively simple but powerful practice. Trataka means "to gaze steadily at a fixed point" and there are two forms of the practice. One is "Bahiranga" or External Trataka—gazing at an object or symbol; "Antaranga" or Internal Trataka—clear and stable inner visualization of an object.

In the practice of Trataka, an object is gazed at until its subtle form manifests in front of the closed eyes. The point of concentration is usually a symbol or an object that activates the inner potential and absorbs the mind. The symbol most commonly used is a candle flame, because even after the eyes are closed, the impression remains naturally for some time, and then Antaranga Trataka can easily be performed. The purpose of focusing the eyes on an external object is to arouse the internal vision and make it steady by stopping the eye movements.

In Trataka the result is a "blanking out" of visual perception, and in the wake of this suspension, the central nervous system begins to function in isolation. When the brain is isolated from the sense modalities and from the

Fig. 65: Trātaka

associated mental process, ideas, memories, etc., triggered by these thought impressions, spiritual consciousness emerges. The higher brain, liberated from time and space, is experienced.

The symbol most commonly used is a candle flame, because even after the eyes are closed, the impression remains naturally for some time, and then antaranga trataka can easily be performed.

There are many other equally effective symbols for Trataka apart from the candle flame, such as a crystal ball, yantra, mandala, chakra, the symbol OM, the Full Moon, a star, the rising or setting Sun (when it is orange, not yellow, at this time the air is particularly rich with the healing prana). These are the most effective, but Trataka can also be done on a rose, a tree, a mountain, the sea, the sky, a rock, a black dot or any object of your choice.

Keep a burning candle at eye level at a distance of one and half feet distance in a meditative posture. Gaze for some time. When you feel any strain on the eyes close them gently. Try to see the after image in the black screen of closed eyes. Practice three times and relax. Observe the effect of this practice. Feel the calmness of mind and easiness of the body.

Nauli

Nauli kindles the digestive fire, removing indigestion, sluggish digestion and all disorders of the doshas, and brings about happiness. (Hatha Yoga Pradipica 2:34)

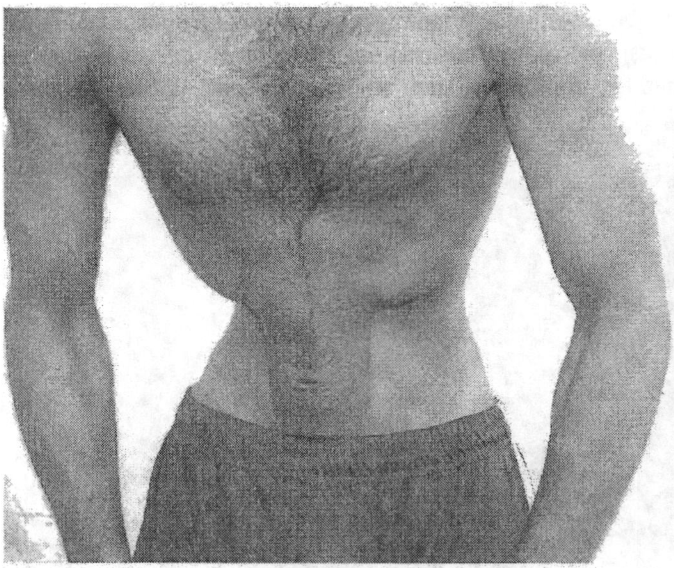

Fig. 66: Nauli

Nauli quickly tones the abdominal muscles, nerves, intestines, reproductive, excretory and urinary organs. Every part of the internal system is stimulated by this practice. It balances the endocrine system and helps to control the production of sex hormones. Nauli is especially useful for alleviating constipation, indigestion, nervous diarrhea, acidity, flatulence, depression, hormonal imbalances, sexual and urinary disorders, laziness, dullness, lack of energy and emotional disturbances. Through its practice one can control sensual desires and strengthen one's willpower.

The Sanskrit "Nauli" comes from the root word "nala" or "nali, which means a tubular vessel, vein or nerve of the body: a reed or hollow stalk. The word "nala" is also the Sanskrit for the rectus abdominii. In the *Gherand Samhita* it is known as "laulika". "Laulika" comes from the word "lola" which means "to roll" or "to agitate". Nauli is the practice of contracting and isolating the rectus abdominii muscles.

"Lean forward, protrude the abdomen and (the muscles) from right to left with speed, this is called Nauli by the siddhas" ("Hatha Yoga Pradipica 2:33)

The rectus abdominii are the two long vertical muscles situated in front of the abdomen, which run from under the centre of the ribcage to the pubic bone. Though these are the muscles you manipulating in Nauli, the external oblique and transverse abdoninii are also used. The muscles are pulled together and the middle group of muscles protrudes: This is Madhyama Nauli. When the rectus abdominii muscles protrude on the left side, it is called Dakshina Nauli. When the muscles protrude on the right side, it is called Vama Nauli. There is also Dynamic Nauli.

This practice is bit advanced. Only Hath-Yogi can do it. For practice it is necessary to gain mastery over Agnisar Kriya and Uddiyan Bandha. Better to practice in standing position. Inhale deeply, exhale forcefully and till forward with the hips as well as tilt the knees and keep the hands over thigh. Contract the abdominal muscles in the centre.

For advanced practitioners it can be churned with outer retention of breath. Release the abdominal muscles, release all parts of the body one by one inhale and relax for a few minutes.

Kapālbhāti

Kapalabhati is the sixth cleansing technique that invigorates the entire brain and awakens the dormant centres responsible for subtle perception. Normal breathing is characterized by active contraction of only the inspiratory muscles, such as the diaphragm and external intercostals. Expiration occurs passively on the cessation of this contraction of the internal intercostals. Kapalabhati reverses this process—exhalation is active while inhalation is passive. This induces a reversal in the flow of the nerve impulses to and from the brain bringing about stimulation and awakening of the brain centers.

The "Gherand Samhita" says that these practices not only get rid of the sinuses of old mucus, but also make one attractive and prevent aging process by relaxing facial muscles and nerves. It rejuvenates tired cells and nerves, keeping the face young, shining and wrinkle free. On the spiritual level these practices stimulate and awake Ajna Chakra.

Sit in padmasana or Vajrasana (with knees separated) and practice rapid exhalation (Like the practice of bhastrika pranayama). Here emphasis will be only on exhalation. Practice ten times and relax for some moments. For more practice, start again. After completing the rounds observe the effects on the abdominal muscles, chest region, throat, nostril and head region.

PRACTICE LEADING TO MEDITATION

Practice of meditation is the one of the important steps of eight fold path of Yoga, guided by Patanjali. Even we find the mention of meditation in Vedic scripts, Upaniśads, Gita and Puranas also. Lord Kṛśna says to Arjuna in thirty fifth verse of the sixth chapter in Gita:

// Asanśayam Mahābhāho Mano Durnigraham Chalam /
/ Abhyāsen tu Kaunteya Vairāgyen Cha Gṛkśate //

Meaning: The mind is restless no doubt and difficult to curb O'Arjuna; But it can be brought under control by repeated practice of meditation and by the exercise of dispassion O' son of Kunti.

Technique 1. Savitā Dhyān

A disciplined mind helps in physical, mental and spiritual will being. There are several techniques of meditation among them ***Savita Dhyan*** (Meditation on rising Sun) is highly effective and beneficial.

Fig. 67: Savitā Dhyan

Pandit Śrīram Sharma Acharya in a *Sadhana* Camp described the practical aspect of Savita Dhyan. In his words: Mental concentration on some gross objects e.g. the rising Sun, is most convenient for majority of people; because, the human mind, in general, is not so developed that it could be focused for a stretch without any visible or perceptible symbol. However with sincere practice, one begins to realize the presence of spirit in his inner self and learn to meditate upon it.

How to practice it? Select a well ventilated calm and clean place for the practice. It will be more effective if the timing is of sunrise. Sit in padmasana, Siddhasana or Sukhasana (simple cross legged) with the spine erect and body parts relaxed. After the body part awareness observe the natural flow of breath. Slowly bring your focus to the center of the brain and try to visualize the light spot of rising Sun. After a few days practice the infusion of light in the brain in the mind should inspire the practitioner to become a witness of all the internal experiences.

Technique 2. So Ham Sadhana

So-ham Sadhana is a technique of meditation to realise the oneness of human consciousness and super consciousness. I am Thou- is the base of this sadhna- the meaning of this mantra. Only due to ignorance we are not able to recognise ourselves. We repeat the mantra with every breath but because of lack of focus we are not able to understand it.

Fig. 68: So Ham Sadhana

Method: Sit in padmāsana, Siddhāsana or Sukhāsana (simple cross legged) with the spine erect and body parts relaxed. Then observe the natural flow of breath. With every inhalation the sound of "So" can be observed and with every exhalation "Ham" sound can be observed. Just watch the breath and feel it. No breath should enter or pass out without your knowledge. The breathing will become slow and the total concentration will be on "So-Ham" mantra. The sound of this mantra is *śāswat*, you don't have to produce. It will come itself. With every inhalation So-o-o and with every exhalation Ham-m-m. The feeling will be I am Thou (This means supreme God, Thou means supreme power, Thou means super consciousness).

Watch the breath, observe the mantra, feel the oneness of soul and body. Concentrate on it for at least ten minutes. The feeling of So-Ham will become stronger (I am Thou) for end the practice slowly remove the awareness from "So-Ham" mantra and observe the outer environment. Move the fingers and toes, hands, legs and neck slowly. Rub the palm and keep on the eyes. Open the eyes slowly.

SPECIAL RELAXATION TECHNIQUE: YOGA NIDRĀ

In the ancient yogic texts Yoga nidra was considered as the ultimate goal of Yoga-Samādhi. Here in the practice of Yoga nidrā it is used as a best technique of relaxation which includes the sleep of body and awakening of consciousness. It is convenient to use Yoga nidrā tape or listen to the instructions of Yoga instructor.

Yoga nidrā has been experienced as "the" most powerful relaxation technique known to man. Yet, in Yoga, it is used much more than that. The power of this technique is such that it is regularly used as a **therapeutic technique** to overcome pain, act on the deepest neurosis and even overcome disability in certain cases.

Fig. 69: Yoga nidra

At its simplest level, it may be understood and practiced as a way of **total physical and mental relaxation**. The advanced benefits can be reached with regular practice. To start with one can follow the spoken instruction of Yoga instructor or it is of course convenient to use Yoga Nidrā Tape. There is a general instruction for Yoga nidrā:

Indian saints and seers have given a beautiful technique of relaxation called Yoga nidra. There are several techniques to relax the body and mind, ***Yoga nidra*** is probably best-known technique to induce complete physical, mental and emotional relaxation. *Yoga nidra* is a state between sleep and *Samadhi*. It is a half sleep and half waking state. The simple and useful practice of the art of sleeping which the yogis know, if proved infinitely beneficial to many people, may be called psychic the sleep.

Yoga nidra is actually an altered state of consciousness. It is neither sleep nor dream nor is it the state of *Samadhi.* The aim of the practice of *Yoga nidra* for the *saints* and *ṛśis* of India was to develop awareness i.e. being aware to the subconscious and unconscious states and ultimately to enter the state of super consciousness.

According to **Maharśi Markandey** *Yoga nidra* is the *state* of deep relaxation as *Lord Visnu* Himself uses this marvelous technique

Utpanneti Tada Loke Sanityapybhidhiyate/
Yoganidram Yada Viśnurjagatyekarnavikṛte//

Maharśi Markandey according to his visualizations states in his text *Markandey Purana* that at the end of *Kalpa* when the entire universe was in a deep relaxation *Lord Viśnu* was lying on the bed of serpent in state of *Yoga nidra.*

Drastwa Tavsurau Chograu prasuptam Cha Janardanam/
Tustav Yoganidram Tamekagrahṛdyasthitih//

Meaning: When *Lord Brahma* observed Him in the state of *Yoga nidra* to make him awake, he started praying Goddess *Yoga nidra* who lives in the eyes of *Lord Viśnu.*

In ancient yog ic text, *Yoga Tadavali*, **Acharya Śankara** described the method of *Yoga nidra* as:

Vichhinn Samkalpa Vikalpa mule, Nihśeś nirmurit karmjale
Nirantarabhyas nitant bhadrasa Jambhrite Yogini Yoga nidra.

Meaning: When mind has transcended maya (delusion), when ego has become static, when senses are no more functioning. And when all communication between the mind and the senses have been cut off when I and you no longer exist for a period of time *Yoga nidra* starts. For a long time practice, when being disappointed with every resolve and imagination and every obstacle of *karma* becomes destroyed, the Yogi gets into the state of *Yoga nidra.*

The author of *Hatha Yoga Pradipika*, great yogi **Swatmarama** classifies *Yoga nidra* as the state of *turiya*; means the all expansive and encompassing 'fourth dimension' in which *Śakti* neither contracts nor expands, but is in union with Śiva or supreme consciousness.

Abhyaset Kheçarim Tavadyavat SyadYoganidṛtah/
SampraptYoganidrasya Kalo Nasti Kadachana//

Meaning: *Khechari* should be practised until yogic sleep occurs. For one who has attained yogic sleep, time become non-existent. Here the term

Yoga nidra has used as the state of *samadhi*. Yogic sleep or *Yoga nidra* is the state in which conscious mind subsides but awareness remains.

Yoga nidra according to **Swami Rama** is a state between sleep and Samadhi. It is a half-sleep and half waking state: it is not a waking state, and it is not really a sleep state. *Yoga nidra* is a state of conscious sleep in which one can record what is going on. There is a fine demarcation between *Yoga nidra* and *samadhi*. In *Yoga nidra* one can record those which he cannot receive in the conscious state. When one cannot register something properly in the waking state, they can go into *Yoga nidra* to register it. *Yoga nidra* is used to develop that wisdom which cannot be developed otherwise. He has divided the practice of Yoga nidra into three phases—in the first phase lie down in *śavasana* and do the sixty-one point exercise. In the second phase there is śithilikaran, and in the last phase, breathe awareness with the visualization of different *charkas* (the different psychic centers of subtle body).

According to **Śrī Ram Sharma Acharya**, *Yoga nidra* can be called scientific sleep. It is a total practice of Yoga it self. The practices of *Sithilasana, Savasana, Sunyavastha and Samadhi* are of great importance in conditioning the body and mind for *Yoganidra*. In usual sleep one does not have any control over his dreams. Autosuggestion is impossible in this case. The practice of *Yoga nidra* on the contrary allows one to attain a state of 'awakened' sleep. In this state, the body and the external mind (and hence the thought process) are made to sleep as per the order of the inner will. The determination, the willpower of the individual self remain active in this state and endeavor auto-suggestive experience of the power of the unconscious mind and its linkage with the soul.

Sw. Satyananda Saraswati explains *Yoga nidra* as a state of mind between wakefulness and dream. When someone practices Yoga nidra he opens the deeper phases of the mind. During the practice of Yoga nidra the consciousness is at different levels. Sometimes it is very close to the senses and at others, it is at a very remote distance. When the consciousness is at a remote distances, then it is only possible to understand through the auditory channels. During Yoga nidra the consciousness is suspended for a few moments periodically, which means that it alternates between the subconscious and unconscious states. Swami Satyanandajee divides Yoga nidra into six steps—preparation, samkalpa (resolve), body part awareness, breath awareness, visualization and ending of the practice.

Hence it is easy to practice. It is of course convenient to use Yoga nidra tape. Health And Yoga News Letters states—*Yoga Nidra* is a superlative relaxation tool. **One hour of effective *Yoga nidra* is equivalent to over 4 hours of sleep.** It is a method of peeling off the subliminal sheath of conscious (external) mind that covers the inner core of the unconscious (inner) mind. In this state the individual consciousness is able to receive the cosmic signals of the super consciousness.

Yoga nidra aims at the removal of the *pratyaya* from the conscious or external plane, the subconscious or subtle plane and the unconscious and causal plane. Thus Yoga nidra can be considered as a highly effective yogic practice to be introduced in the society for a healthy and happy mind.

Preparation: Lie down in śavasana with legs apart and hands beside the body while palm facing upward. Head neck and spine should be in one line. Close your eyes and relax the body. During the practice of Yoga nidra you don't have to fall in sleep and don't have to move the body.

Just feel that you are in complete rest for sleep but don't sleep. Observe the body parts, observe the bodily condition and observe the outer environment. Observe the sounds coming from outside the room.

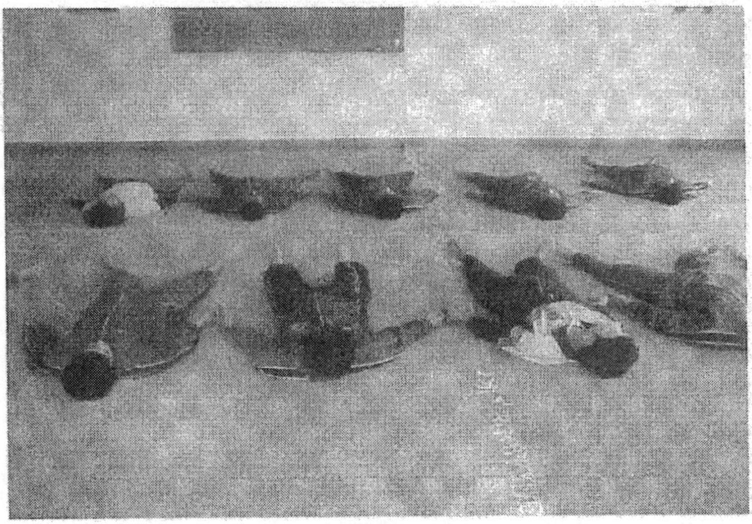

Fig. 70: Yoga Nidrā

Samkalpa: The practice includes resolution (samkalpa). Take a positive resolution related to the goal of life. Repeat it three times mentally. Resolution should be short and simple.

Rotation of Consciousness: Now start rotating your awareness of body parts. Start with right side of the body right hand thumb, index finger, middle finger, ring finger, little finger, palm, back of the palm, right wrist, fore arm, elbow, upper arm, shoulder, armpit, right side chest, waist, right hip, right thigh, knee, ankle, right big toe, second toes, third toe, forth toe, fifth toe the whole right side. Bring the awareness to the left side of the body—left hand thumb, index finger, middle finger, ring finger, little finger, palm, back of the palm, left wrist, fore arm, elbow, upper arm, shoulder, armpit, left side chest, waist left side hip, left thigh, knee, ankle, left big toe, second toe, third toe, forth toe, fifth toe the whole left side of the body. Bring awareness now to the back part of the body—both the soles, heels, calf muscles, back of the knees, back of the thighs, both the buttocks, hip joint, lower back, upper back, spine, shoulder blades, back of the neck, back of the head. Bring awareness to the front part of the body. Top of the head, fore head, eyebrows, eyes, ears, nostrils, chicks, lips, chin, throat, chest, upper abdomen, lower abdomen, hip joint, thighs, knee cap, shin bone, feet, the whole front part of the body. Once the whole body together.

Breath Awareness: Bring the awareness now to your breath, no any change in breathing pattern. Just watch the natural breath. Observe the movement at abdominal region, the navel comes up and goes down. Just count down the breath starting from 23 and reach up to zero. No hurry and no mistake. If you forget the number again start from twenty three. Be aware that you are practicing Yoga nidrā, don't fall asleep. Be aware of the breath, be aware of the number.

Visualisation: Leave the awareness of breath, start visualising the things as per instruction—Just feel that the body weight is increasing and you are becoming heavy, pause, just feel that the body weight is loosing and you are becoming light weighted, pause, feel the coolness of the environment, pause, feel the hotness of the environment. Try to visualise the rising sun, pause, the candle flame, pause, the full moon, pause, the stars in the sky, pause................. Heavy raining..... Red clouds..... The Flying birds..... Endless desert..... Deep well..... Small garden..... Sea burning fire..... 'Om'..... Statue of Lord Buddha.... Mahakāl......

Samkalpa: Let the visualization end; repeat the resolution three times again. Repeat the same samkalpa with full faith.

Ending: Start moving the toes and fingers, hands, legs and neck. Move the body slowly turn to the left and come up into seated position with eyes closed. Rub the palm and keep it on the eyes. Open eyes slowly. Yoga Nidrā ends.

Yoga Nidrā is a superlative relaxation tool. One hour of effective Yoga nidrā is equivalent to over 4 hours of sleep. But, the true purpose of Yoga nidra goes well beyond deep relaxation. Yoga Nidrā establishes the link between the conscious desires, the will power, the subconscious and the unconscious mind. When this happens you reap all-round powerful benefits and feel in total control of all aspects of life.

Index

Abdominal organs, 50, 141
Anti-insulin actions, 78
Anxiety, 2, 47, 115, 119–20, 160
Ardhaśalabhāsana, 149
Ardhtatali, 129
Arteriosclerosis, 73–74, 85
Arthritis, 73–74, 81, 85
Ashwini mudras, 51
Aspirant of yoga, 98, 121
Astakumbhaka, 41
Astānga Namaskār, 136
Astanga Yoga, 19, 37, 56–58
Asthma, 74, 79, 86–87
Astigmatism, 160
Astral body, 74
Aśwāsanchālan, 135, 137
Atharva Veda, 15, 95
Atma Nivedan, 31
Atreya, S.K., 14
Attention Deficit Disorder, 93
Audio-visual aids, 108, 113, 116
Aurobindo, Śri, 7, 24
Austerity, 11, 57
Axial skeleton, 60
Ayurveda, 47, 81

Batra, B.K., 3
Bhagvad Purana, 21
Bhagwad Gita, 17, 19, 28, 30
Bhakti Cult, 22
Bhakti Yoga, 17, 24, 28
Bhakti, types of, 32
Bhastrikā, 156
Bhrāmari, 155
Bhujangāsana, 136, 148
Bihar School of Yoga, 22, 48
Blood circulation, 85, 125, 127, 131–32, 139, 150
Blood glucose, 77–78
Blood pressure, 47–48, 74, 78, 125
Blood vessels, 62, 66, 85
Body weight, 73, 87, 106, 170
Breath awareness, 74, 77, 133, 147–48, 168, 170
Breath control, 57, 153–54
Buddhi, 7, 50, 52

Calf muscles, 127–28, 139–40, 142, 144, 146, 153, 170
Candle flame, 160–61, 170
Cardiovascular disorders, 125
Chakki Chālāsana, 142
Chitta Vritti, 52
Chronic fatigue, 73–74
Circulatory system, 62, 66, 76–77
Class Management, 100, 110
Consciousness
    creativity of, 9
    individual, 6, 10, 29, 52, 76, 88, 168
    super, 165, 167–68
    supreme, 6, 12, 71, 167
    universal, 29, 56, 71
Constipation, 75, 81–82, 162
Cycling, 86, 140

Dandāsana, 135
Defecation, 82–83, 160
Degenerative chronic disorders, 1
Demonstration Method, 103
Dhanurāsana, 148

Dhauti, 40, 42, 158–60
Dhyan, Practice of, 41
Diabetes, 74, 77–78, 85, 87
Diaphragm, 50, 65, 163
Difficult students, dealing with, 111
Digestive systems, 48, 61, 65–66, 82, 86
Directed-practice method, 102
Disorder symptoms start, 80

Ear-throat-nose systems, 158
Educational principles, 108
Endocriner systems, 48, 64, 66, 74, 162
Epic period, 16
Epidermis, 62
Evolutionary psychology, 67
Examofobia, 2
Excretory (urinary) system, 63
Extra-class practice, 114

Fatty tissue, 106

Ganguly, S.K., 3
Gāyatri Mantra, 3
Gene-environment interaction, 67
Genito-excretory systems, 45
Gharote, M.L., 3
Gheranda Samhita, 22, 40, 42–46, 49, 51, 162–63
Gheranda, Maharśi, 40
Gomukhāsana, 151
Grivā Sanchālan, 132
Gulf Ghurnan, 127
Gulf Naman, 132
Gurukula system, 1

Hastotthānāsana, 134, 138
Hatha Yoga Pradipika, 39, 41–46, 48, 167
Hatha Yoga, 22–24, 35, 39–43, 45, 158
Hathayogic practices, 22
Health psychology, 67
Healthy life style, 84
Heart disease, 47, 79, 83, 85–87
Hiranyagarbha, 13–14
Hormone systems, 44
Hypertension, 48, 76–77, 79, 83, 87

Immune systems, 65–66
Individualized Instructional Method, 102
Induced ailments, 71–72
Insulin, 78
Integumentary systems, 62

Jainism, 19–20
Jal Neti, 76–77, 81
Jalandhar Bandha, 41, 46, 48, 50
Jānu Chakra, 128
Jānu Falak Akarśan, 128
Jānu naman, 127
Jnana Yoga, 17, 24
JñānYogi, 26
Jung's Theory of Archetypes, 8
Kapalbhati, 40, 42–43, 74, 158, 163
Karma Yoga, 17, 24, 32–33, 35, 88–89
  Sadhana of, 34
Karma Yogi, 34
Kaśmir Śaivism, 24
Kāsthatakśanāsana, 143
Katichakrāsana, 145
Kehuni Naman, 131
Kriya Yoga, 37, 55
Kriyamana Karma, 32
Krśnamacharya, T., 23
Kumbhaka, 46, 48
Kundalini, 36, 39, 45–47, 49–51

LaghūSankha Prakśālana, 160
Law of karma, 32–33
Lecture method, 101
Lesson plan, 114–114
Lunar plexus, 50

Madhu Bhumika, 38
Mahabhasya, 12
Maharshi Patanjali, 55
Maharśi, Raman, 24
Mandukyopanishad, 53
Manibandha Chakra, 131
Mantra-Chudamanyopniśad, 35
Manusmrti, 20
Mārjariāsana, 150
Medieval Period (Tantra Stage), 21
Meditation, 20, 163
  characteristics of, 119
  method of teaching, 120
Meditative postures, 147, 154–56, 161

Meditative, cultural and relaxation *asana*, 139
Methods of Teaching, 100
Mind management, 23
Model Lesson Plan, 114
Modern Period, 22
Moola Bandha, 51
Motor activities, 106, 113
Motor skills, 106, 108
Mudra, 41
Mudra-bandha, 49
Mula bandhas, 49, 51
Muladhara Chakra, 39
Mumuksutva (longing for liberation), 27
Muscular system, 60, 65
Mustikā Bandha, 130

Nadi Shodhan Pranayama, 46
Nādiśodhan, 154
Nagratna, R., 3
Narada Bhakti Sutra, 28
Natha Cult, 22
Natrājāsana, 152
Naukachālāsana, 143
Naukāsana, 149
Nauli, 161, 162
Nervous system, 44, 48–49, 63, 150, 161
Neti, 158–159
Northern School of Yoga, 23

Obesity, 78, 80
Obsessive-Compulsive Disorder (OCD), 73
Orthopedic disorders, 86
Osteoporosis, 85–86, 88
Out-of-class practices, 102

Pād Chakrāsana, 140
Pād Sanchālan, 140, 141
Pādanguli Naman, 126, 132
Padhastāsana, 134, 138
Padmasana, 41, 74, 146, 163–64
Parvatāsana, 137
Paschimottanasana, 41, 74, 147
Patanjal Yoga, introduction to, 54
Patanjali Yoga Sutra, 6, 13, 36–37, 40, 52, 54, 56–58
Patanjali Yoga system, 19
Patanjali, Maharśi, 6, 12, 36
Pathogenic organisms, 62
Pauranic Stage, 21
Pedagogic practice, 123
Peristaltic activities, 66
Personality
  concept of, 95
  development of, 95
Physiological Principles, 106
Pranāmāsana, 133, 139
Pranavidya, 15
Pranayama, 1, 3, 19–21, 37, 40–43, 45–50, 66, 74–75, 77, 79, 97–98, 105, 120, 153–54
Pranic energy, 45, 56–58, 72, 79
Preparatory practices, 125
Pre-Vedic Period, 14
Prevention and management of diseases, 1
Pristha Sanchālan, 142
Progressive part method, 109
Project Method, 103
Psychological principles, 105
Psycho-motor coordination, 1
Punctuality, 121–22
Purification or *Śatkarma*, 40
Pūrnatitali, 129

Raja Yoga, 24, 35–38
Raja Yogi, kinds of, 38
Reproductive system, 64
Respiratory system, 62, 64, 66, 79
Response-to-Instruction Method, 102
Rgveda, 14–15

Sadhaka, 27, 38, 40
Sadhana Camp, 164
Sadhana of Vedanta, 27
Sajjan Dharma, 31
Śakti-worship, 21
Śalabhāsana, 149
Samadhi, 36
Sanchita Karma, 32
Saptanga Yoga, 40
Sarvāngāsana, 152
Śatkarma practice, 158
Satsampati (Six-attainments), 27
Satsanga, 29

Śavāsana, 153
Savita Dhyan, 164
Scientific psycho-spiritual discipline, 1
Self-awareness, 57, 73, 133
Selfless actions, 33
Shatkarma, 42–43
Siddhasana, 41, 44, 74, 145, 164
Simhāsana, 150
Śitali, 157
Śitkāri, 157
Śiva, 12
Sivananada, Swami, 24
Skandh Chakra, 132
Skeletal systems, 59–60, 65–66, 73
Skin disorders, 86
Smrti Period, 20
So Ham Sadhana, 165
Social Adaptation parameters, 3
Sociological Principles, 110
Sources of Teaching Method, 105
Spinal misalignments, 72
Spinal nerves, 63
Spine erect, 145–47, 154–55, 164–65
Spiritual awakening, 41, 45, 145–47
Spiritual bodies, 24, 74
Spiritual path, 42–43
Spiritual self, 89–90
Spiritual values, 92
Sravana, 26–27
Śri Ram Charita Manasa, 29
Śriram Sharma Acharya, 24
Śroni Chakra, 130
Sukhāsana, 147
Surya Namaskar, 74, 133
Suryabhedan, 79–80, 156
Sutra Period, 18
Swatmarama, Swami, 39–40, 46–48
Swastikasana, 21, 41, 146

Tādāsana, 144
Taimni, I.K., 18
Tantra Yoga, 24
Tantrism, 22
Teacher-centered approach, 101
Teaching-Learning, Scope of, 91
Tellcs S., 3
Thoreau, Henry, 17
Thyroid disorders, 80
Tiryaktādāsana, 144
Transcendent consciousness, 8
Trātaka, 160, 161
Tulsi Das, Goswami, 11, 29

Udarākarśan, 141
Uddiyana Bandha, 41, 50
Ujjai, 155
Uma, K., 3
Undue tension, 107
Universal law, 32
Upaniśadic Period, 15
Urinary disorders, 162
Urinary systems, 63–64
Utility value, 110
Uttānpādāsana, 139

Vairagya (dispassion), 26
Vaman Dhauti, 159
Vata disorder, 81
Vedanta psychology, 68
Vedic Period, 15
Vedic yoga, advantage of, 9
Vipreet karnee āsana, 151
Visceral muscles, 61
Visual demonstration, 108, 113
Viveka (Discrimination), 26
Viveka Gyan, 56
Vivekananda, Swami, 22, 24, 32
Vomiting, 159–60
Vyaśa, Maharśi, 13

Western psychology, 67
World Health Organization, 89

Yagavalkya, Maharśi, 13
Yama, 21, 37, 43, 56–57, 153
Yoga
- arthritis and, 81
- asthma and, 79
- basic principles of, 105
- camps, 100
- diabetes mellitus and, 77
- digestive disorder and, 82
- disease and health in, 71
- in education, 91
- education and moral values, 93
- healthy lifestyle and, 88